World Soul

Healing Ourselves and the Earth Through Pagan Theology

Catherine Carr

Stella Luma Press

Copyright © 2023 Catherine Carr All rights reserved.

No part of this publication may be reproduced, distributed, or transmitted without the prior written permission of the publisher, except as permitted by fair use rules for review or criticism under U.S. copyright law.

For permission to quote, to order books in bulk, or to request a speaking engagement, contact:

catherinecarrspirit@gmail.com

Book cover by GetCovers.com

ISBN: 979-8-9850761-2-7

Contents

Introduction	IV
A Note On Sources	VII
1. What Makes Paganism Different?	1
2. What is a God? The Answer May Surprise You.	23
3. On the Sacredness of Life	34
4. The Web of Life, the Divine Family	52
5. Pagan Ethics and Values	66
6. Pagan Gender Theology	82
7. How Do Destructive Theological Ideas Arise?	101
8. Building a Better World on Pagan Theology	121
9. Love This Book?	133
10. Acknowledgements	134
11. About the Author	136

Introduction

Pagan theology offers a fundamentally different theological perspective from other major religions that are popular in the West. Although the term "Paganism" covers tens of thousands of different regional traditions, all lack certain theological assumptions which have been instrumental in shaping imperial theologies and philosophies for the past two thousand years, and which have played a major role in the development of today's humanitarian and environmental crises.

Modern Pagan communities present a unique opportunity because they are often built around both modern moral and ethical frameworks such as harm vs. care ethics, consent culture, rational values, and ancient wisdom which indigenous cultures have used to keep their people in the right relationship with the ecosystems they depend on for survival.

Pagan views on the sacredness of life, the role of humanity in the web of life, and the relationship of individuals to the Divine provide powerful protocols and theological frameworks for prioritizing humanitarian and environmental issues in order to undo the damage done by destructive theological ideas over the course of recent centuries. Many of these ideas are at some level compatible with the theologies of other religions, but have taken a back seat due to the presence of other teachings which compete or conflict with these values and practices.

It is time for Pagans and non-Pagans alike to re-examine many of their religion's teachings and ask if their religions are falling prey to theological ideas which prioritize the profit of the powerful over the sanctity of life; and if their religious practices are sufficient to encourage the behavioral changes we need to make to save the world for our children and grandchildren.

For this reason, I have written this book with an eye, not just for students of Paganism, but for students and teachers of other faiths. If you are Pagan, my goal is to answer your questions about why Paganism feels so different from so many other religions, and equip you to explain what you have experienced firsthand to those who ask. If you are not Pagan, it is my hope that the perspectives here will give you food for thought when addressing problems such as climate change and environmental destruction, sustainability, sexism, sexuality, and issues of gender identity with your congregations.

Pagans describe their religions as life-affirming and validating, welcoming to religious experiences that are rejected by other religious groups. In many cases Pagans are former followers of another religion who came to Paganism after discovering that their religious community did not seem to have room for their religious experiences or their sense of right and wrong. I argue that modern Pagan communities are doing a better job of addressing the humanitarian and environmental crises we face precisely because they lack certain theological preconceptions that have dominated Western religion for the past two millennia.

Together we will see that there is a better way of living. We will discuss practices which are common in some modern Pagan communities and which are successful in mitigating the effects of prejudice, discrimination, and oppression; and practices which are successful in cultivating a deep, abiding love of our fellow species which motivate resistance to destructive economic activities.

This book has been a long time coming. It has been in my mind to write a book which clarifies why I became Pagan, and why I believe the religion of my birth was failing to address today's human rights and humanitarian crises, for at least a decade. But this proved extraordinarily difficult to do within a reasonable page count. Like the web of life we will discuss, all things in life are interwoven to the point of being almost one. This turns out to mean that Aquinas's *Summa Theologica* is so long because, once you start discussing one subject in theology, you almost have to discuss them all. I have done my best here to produce a book for people who are new to Pagan theology as a formal study which covers the most important bases within a page count that a reader can consume in an afternoon if they so choose.

I have brought clinical data to bear to support the theological claims made here, as is my penchant, and the reader is encouraged to explore those scientific findings which are linked in the footnotes. Many other uncited claims come to me through my decade of personal experience moving within the modern Pagan communities of North America.

Why should polytheists have a theological edge over monotheists when it comes to many human rights issues? Why should animists have a practical advantage when it comes to addressing environmental crises? And what is a "god" anyway? Have some religions been using the word "God" to refer to two drastically different and mutually exclusive concepts?

Come with me and we will get a fresh perspective on God, the natural world, and humanity's relationship with both.

A Note On Sources

In a great many cases I have made claims about theological ideas without citing them. This is generally because these ideas either represent oral traditions that I have been personally exposed to but which do not derive from published source texts, or because there are so many different sources from different religious traditions making the same claim that citing them all would be impossible.

In cases where I have cited specific sources, it is usually in the interest of providing representative examples of ideas which the reader may not have encountered before for the reader's closer examination. These sources have often been chosen for ease of free access so that the reader may begin digging deeper into a train of religious thought from anywhere in the world, rather than because they are the most authoritative or comprehensive treatment of their topics.

Since much of what is discussed in this book speaks of what people today *do* believe, rather than what academic experts or holy books say they *should* believe, prioritizing accessibility of sources and opinions of people who are influential in the popular digital information sphere over scholarly assessments and theories seemed appropriate.

For those readers who may find some of the academic articles which are cited to be paywalled, it is useful to know that as of this writing, JSTOR is still offering free memberships to individuals which allow the free reading of up to 100 of the database's scholarly articles per month. This relatively recent offering is well worth looking into if you have an interest in scholarly research on any topic, and was of tremendous assistance to the writing of this book.

Lastly, I want to apologize for being unable in many cases to give indigenous peoples the credit they deserve for the development and maintenance of many of the helpful ideas and pieces of information presented herein. I had a truly disturbing amount of trouble finding written sources about indigenous teachings whose authenticity and accuracy I had a high degree of confidence in, so I restricted many of my statements about indigenous beliefs to vague references to general cross-cultural trends instead of attempting to make statements about the teachings of specific indigenous peoples. I hope to be able to change this in future books and offer more of you the credit that you deserve.

People with information they think I should know about, or who wish to be quoted or educate me on an issue relevant to the contents of this book are welcome to email catherinecarrspirit@gmail.com. More books on topics related to those discussed here are planned, and I will take all the help I will get in accessing knowledge of boots-on-the-ground religious practices, beliefs, and oral traditions I might not otherwise have access to.

Thank you all for reading. I hope this book gives you something.

Chapter One

What Makes Paganism Different?

What makes Paganism feel fundamentally different to its followers when compared to many other religions? Why does it seem so welcoming to people who may have been rejected by other religions because of their religious experiences, gender, or sexuality? How do the attitudes which allow this sense of homecoming for so many also facilitate greater respect for biological life and the autonomy of human beings than what is found in many other religious communities today?

Some would argue that other religious communities offer these same benefits, but for many Pagans, they came to Paganism only after being rejected by or failing to fit in with one or more other religious traditions. They were told that their gender, sexuality, religious experiences, or spiritual practices were wrong and unacceptable to God; or they felt unseen and unrepresented within religious communities which acted dismissive of their experiences and their views on matters of central moral and ethical importance.

So why is Paganism able to accommodate religious experiences and religious views that struggle to find homes in many other religions? And why do so many Pagans feel that Pagan beliefs and practices hold humanity to a higher moral standard than many of the religions they have left?

The answers to these questions are found somewhat in teachings which all religions share, but also in the *absence* of teachings within Paganism that are found in many patriarchal and imperial faiths. Modern Pagans, by harkening both to the pre-colonial past and to the cutting-edge moral developments of today, are able to build religious communities which prioritize life first and foremost without conflicting or distracting teachings found in many other religious communities.

So what teachings do other religions popular in the West have that modern Paganism *doesn't* have? Which of these assumptions are felt and practiced in many patriarchal and imperial religions, even if they are not explicitly spelled out in their theology? And where do these assumptions come from, if they're not actually rooted in the depths of theology?

We'll explore all of that throughout this book. But for now, let's take on some theological ideas you may have heard and see how they're harming our people and our fellow species. Later in this book, we'll see what alternatives to these ideas look like in practice, and discuss some protocols for removing these potentially harmful ideas from our religious communities and practices.

#1 God is Male

This belief is an interesting one in that some religions explicitly teach it, while others only seem to believe it subconsciously. And this is an interesting clue as to this idea's source: it comes from the subconscious biases of patriarchal society, more than from any divine revelation or pure logic.

I have rarely spoken to a theologian of any religion who genuinely believed that God was a man. Nearly all religions explicitly teach that God transcends and encompasses all human genders. This is true of most strains of Christianity, Islam, Judaism, Hinduism, Zoroastrianism and every other religion whose theologians I have spoken with. In fact, in the original languages of most of these religions, one can see that care has been taken to refer to God and humanity in ways that indicate both masculine and feminine gender, or no gender at all.

Jewish scriptures variously describe God as a genderless spirit, as a male warrior, and as a birthing mother. The founding theologians of Christianity and Islam continued the Jewish view that God transcends and encompasses all genders, and the Zoroastrian name of God, Ahura Mazda, consists of both masculine and feminine parts. It is taught that this is necessary and important to avoid giving the impression that one gender is closer to God than the other.

Yet these careful linguistic choices have not survived in translations of many of these sacred texts into modern languages. We'll discuss *why* this happens so universally more in Chapter 7, but for now skeptics may wish to dig into the original theology and language around God's gender in their tradition.

The result of this masculinization of God over time has been that many laypeople and some theologians of these religions believe that the Creator of the Universe is literally of the male sex or gender, despite the obvious logical problems with this idea. Many followers of Christianity and Islam, for example, believe that the gendered pronouns used to refer to God are literally true, and that any suggestion that God is not literally male are feminist propaganda.

In many cases this depiction of God as male has also resulted in the idea that among humans, only men are capable of mediating between God and humanity as priests, of performing certain vital spiritual operations, or of performing certain duties of leadership. Many world religions still insist that women are incapable of performing priestly and pastoral responsibilities.

With these ideas swimming around, it is no wonder that the rights of women and other genders have been steadily whittled away in many world religious systems over the past few thousand years. It is also no wonder that many religious leaders of today consider moves to increase women's legal rights and economic power to be in active conflict with the maintenance of their religious traditions, making these religious traditions active proponents of oppression and active facilitators of violence against people who aren't cisgender men.

Nor are violations of the rights of women and other genders the only negative consequence of conceptualizing God only as a man. This idea is also linked to some truly disturbing theologies which feature prominently in the most violent and oppressive religious movements of today.

The most disturbing view of God as a man pictures him not as a nurturing father, but as a slave owner who is entitled to demand anything He likes of humans, and to punish them in any way He likes. This view is common in religions which teach that people who disobey God's will go to Hell, and according to the tradition of Goddess theologians, is related to the idea of God as male.

The logic goes like this: the most logical way to envision God, if we must assign God a single gender, is as a mother. Among humans, only women can create new life, and they do it by giving birth of their own flesh and blood.

If humans are in any way divine in nature, then, it makes more sense to imagine them being birthed by God through such a loving and tender sharing of Her essence than to imagine them being made of an inferior, separate substance as is common in creation stories featuring gods as male craftsmen.

Without any involvement of any birth-giving form of God, these Pagan theologians argue, it is impossible for God to have a truly familial relationship with humanity. Indeed, just such a depiction of God as a birthing mother is found in Jewish and Christian scripture (a list of Biblical descriptions of God as female is included in this footnote for those interested),[1] but this depiction is so rarely discussed by today's Christian religious teachers that many Christians do not even know that such imagery exists in the Bible.

In the most pathological strains of patriarchal religion, this total lack of familial affinity between God and humanity is indeed what we see. Strains of Christianity and Islam exist in which humans are viewed as God's slaves or tools; unconditionally obligated to follow God's instructions and unconditionally subject to any punishment or torture God may choose to mete out.

The idea that God is the craftsman who made humanity and now has rights to us as property is one of the ideas fueling violent religious extremism in the world today. People still exist who will tell you that

---

1. Female images of god in the Bible. Women's Ordination Conference. https://www.womensordination.org/resources-old/female-images-of-god-in-the-bible/

God is justified in burning nonbelievers in Hell for eternity—and that by extension religious leaders are justified in forcing conversions and violently punishing sinners and nonbelievers in an effort to prevent this.

I've spoken to such believers on numerous occasions. They are often the same people who find the idea of women in positions of religious leadership to be morally dangerous.

Whether this criminally bleak view of God and humanity is a direct result of the removal of the Goddess from modern religious theology, or a comorbid symptom of the motivations we will discuss in Chapter 7 is uncertain.

One solution proposed by Pagan Goddess theologians is that conceptualizing and referring to God as female could do a great deal to alleviate humanitarian and environmental disasters.

Their argument is a compelling one: that envisioning God as a nurturing mother in relationship with creations born from Her own flesh, blood, and spirit, doing violence against fellow humans and the natural world may become more difficult to theologically justify. Some Goddess theologians even propose that the increasing masculinization of God over the past few millennia has been done specifically to provide increasing justification for wars of greed. Painting God as a conquering war leader who is admirable because of His destructive power, after all, makes it much easier to justify violence against your fellow living beings than portraying God as a nurturing mother who birthed these beings from Her own body.[2]

---

2. Sjöö, M., & Mor, B. (2012). The Great Cosmic Mother: Rediscovering The Religion of the Earth. HarperOne, an imprint of HarperCollinsPublishers.

Some modern Pagan theologians caution that the replacement of a hypermasculine God with a hyper feminine Goddess may come with its own host of humanitarian limitations, and that contemplation of God as encompassing all genders, not just the traditionally feminine, is necessary to truly restore balance to our world. But restoring a view of God as encompassing all genders is likely a step in the right direction toward re-prioritizing the divine value of life and de-prioritizing war and violence as means of asserting moral authority.

For Pagans, portraying God as male, female, and additional genders is not a struggle. Most Pagan pantheons include deities of at least male and female genders, and frequently also deities who appear to meet the descriptions of genderfluid, nonbinary, or agender as well. This is a reflection of the Pagan instinct that divinity and perfection cannot all be contained in a single anthropomorphic form; many gods are necessary because the divine behaves and relates to humanity in ways that transcend any individual human relationship.

Pagan pantheons, then, like many indigenous pantheons, include Earth Mothers who give birth to all life from their own bodies, the soil; Sky Fathers who physically fertilize the Earth with rain; and spirits who change or transcend genders in a reminder of the fluidity and kinship of all genders.

We will learn much more about this in Chapter 6, but for now consider the implications of Goddess as Mother, and of God as nonbinary or genderfluid. You may find that contemplating this reality changes your instincts on a number of matters for the better.

If you are someone who has already had visions of Goddesses, then welcome home. It was my own vision of a Goddess which began my journey into Paganism, and I can confirm that you are in the right place.

#2 Humans Are Superior to Other Beings

In many strains of Christianity, humans are considered unique among living beings in our theological importance. Some churches explicitly teach that plants, animals, and all natural resources were created for no reason other than to be useful and pleasing to humans, and some even characterize advocates for environmental conservation and animal rights as heretical idolaters.

This objectification and commodification of other living beings has contributed to the idea that unlimited ecological destruction is theologically justified, or even morally good, if it is construed as "being fruitful and multiplying" as God orders Adam and Eve to do in Genesis. It has also contributed to the systematic extermination of indigenous religions and the demonization of ecological activists.

This idea is found most explicitly in Christianity, but is also present in Islam. Both religions teach that only humans have divine souls which are capable of eternal salvation, and that any spirits which appear to belong to plants, animals, landforms, or other natural phenomena are to be viewed with profound suspicion as being potentially evil entities.

The logic goes like this: since both religions permit worship *only* of the Supreme God, any spirits in the natural world which appear amenable to any form of offering, sacrifice, ritual, or veneration are guilty of promoting idolatry. In fact, these spirits are likely to be either demons or demonically influenced. And any human beings who engage in spiritual relationships with other species, landforms, weather systems, or other natural entities can be assumed to be guilty of "demonism," the worship of demons.

This logic is so pervasive that false charges of animism were among the methods historically used by Christian teachers to attempt to demonize Islam, and the same equation of animism to demonism was used to eradicate indigenous religions by Christian and Muslim missionaries and the beginning of the use of the term "Pagan" as a slur indicating a wicked or immoral person.

The idea that all people who believed that plants or animals had spirits or theological significance were under the influence of malicious evil spirits played a role in the idea that such people were savage, uneducated, and untrustworthy, and were in need of being "saved" by missionaries who would preach on the "evils" of such beliefs and tell people they must repent and renounce them or go to Hell.

Fast forward to the early 21st century, when we are realizing that the very existence of our communities is threatened by the extent to which the species we rely on for our own survival have been poisoned and depleted by people who believed these beings had no divine nature or theological importance.

This idea that the supremacy of humans and their God precludes the attribution of ensoulment or theological importance to other species is still used by some Christian and Muslim traditions today. These groups have managed to have a profoundly negative impact on human rights, environmental conservation, and religious rights.

Too many missionaries still refer to all religions which acknowledge the existence of plant, animal, or land spirits as "demonism." Some encyclopedias produced by Christian religious organizations to this day still describe the gods and companion spirits of virtually all indigenous religions as "demons" and characterize them as malicious and coercive in their relations with humanity.[3]

---

3. Shamanism. Catholic Encyclopedia: Shamanism. https://www.newadvent.org/cathen/13750a.htm

The same charges of "demonism" and "idolatry" are also being actively used to demonize ecological activists in the West by Christian and Muslim religious leaders who claim that their love of the Earth is "excessive" and constitutes a betrayal of the One True God who is the only rightful recipient of such love.[4]

The argument that ecological activism is in inherent conflict with Christian theology and is espoused by malicious people who wish to destroy Christian communities is common today on the American political right, where it is used to paint support for politicians who will allow corporations unfettered rights to environmental destruction as a moral obligation for all Christians.

For Pagans, the teaching on plant, animal, land, and weather spirits is much different. Humans since time immemorial have experienced our fellow beings as alive, ensouled, and divine. Any theology which treats the world as the world of God's hands must include our fellow living and natural beings within this definition. To countless individuals in the world today, the restriction of ensoulment, theological importance, and worship to humans and their One God seems arbitrary and unnatural.

Indeed, one of the leading reasons people report converting to Paganism is the feeling that their religious experiences involving nature, plants, or animals were not welcome in their home religion. This was true of me, who always experienced my most intense religious ecstasies and visions in nature and involving natural imagery. Yet I was told by my home church that it was wrong and idolatrous of me to regard my

---

4. Clauson, K. L.. Environmentalism: A Modern Idolatry. Reformed.org. https://reformed.org/webfiles/antithesis/v1n2/ant_v1n2_environ.html

fellow species and divine creations as having souls or spirits, and that it was wrong to cultivate spiritual relationships with them.

In Paganism, there is no such prohibition. Indeed, the core belief of Pagan religions is that the world is divinely created, and that humans are only one of the many theologically significant ensouled beings who inhabit it. The knowledge of indigenous faiths that we are only part of an interdependent web of life spontaneously arises again and again in the religious experiences of individuals—if they are not told by their churches and mosques that these experiences are wrong, idolatrous, or even demonic.

If you have had such an experience, welcome. You will find good company in Pagan communities, who acknowledge the existence of many more spiritual beings than are acknowledged by some other world religions, and who see the potential for healing ourselves and our world in cultivating relationships with them.

In the cases of religions where the desire to be a faithful servant of God is actively pitted against the desire to value, nourish, and protect fellow living beings, we can know that a theology has truly failed.

The idea of attributing real theological importance and divine nature to other species can be frightening, because we have built an economic system which is so dependent on the exploitation and destruction of plants and animals. But those of us who are paying attention are aware that these same practices have already caused massive humanitarian crises, with the number of people who are displaced and facing starvation due to ecological calamities rising each year.

The only thing we can say for sure about the modern era is that, if we continue our current practices, the result will be profound suffering and potentially mass death for our grandchildren. We know that things have been steadily getting worse for years, and every shred of logic and evidence suggests that this will continue until our behavior toward our fellow living and divinely created beings changes.

Perhaps, then, it is time to reconsider what constitutes idolatry and what constitutes good stewardship. Perhaps it is time to seriously consider whether prioritizing our fellow species and our natural surroundings in our theologies and religious practices is necessary.

#3 God is Jealous

The Abrahamic monotheisms are, as far as I know, unique among modern world religions in postulating that the Creator of the Universe is capable of experiencing jealousy. While some Abrahamic theologians may disagree with this assessment and say that descriptions of God as jealous are mere metaphors for the aid of human understanding, many of their own fellow theologians would disagree with them.

Pagan gods do experience jealousy, but the conceptual differences between a Pagan "god" and a monotheistic God are crucial to understand here. These differences, which we will discuss more in Chapter 2, mean that Pagan views on moral authority, ethics, and worship are fundamentally different from the monotheistic view.

Don't get me wrong—Pagan gods can and do get jealous. But their jealousy is treated as a vice, *not* a commandment with moral authority. In other words, if Zeus is jealous that you are paying too much attention to some living being or some other god, that's Zeus's problem. Not yours.

This approach is necessary in a polytheistic system where divine attributes are split between multiple gods. A god's jealousy is not a moral good if they are jealous of a fellow god whose claim to moral authority, theological importance, and worship is just as strong as their own. Jealousy is understood by Pagans as a consequence of the insecurity of finite beings, whether it appears in a human or a god. Jealousy and other vices on the part of Pagan gods, then, are not generally used to make moral or religious policy within Pagan communities.

Something different seems to have happened in the evolution of the monotheistic idea of God. In this view, since there is only one absolute moral authority, and only one being who can be properly worshiped, jealousy becomes a valid moral law. Actions which may make God jealous become vices, including the "vices" of acknowledging other living beings or other names and faces of God as deserving of reverence.

On the face of it, this is logically very odd. Most people know, at some level, that jealousy is a manifestation of insecurity. Jealousy occurs when there is genuine concern that a person might lose something that they feel they need due to attention or other resources being paid to another person. How, then, can a God who is genuinely infinite, omnipotent, and omniscient genuinely be jealous? How can such a God genuinely *need* humanity's attention, or genuinely *fear* being replaced?

This logical contradiction is the reason why many monotheistic theologians now teach that the "jealousy" God describes Himself as having in their scriptures is actually a metaphor. According to these strains of monotheistic theology, God does not actually experience jealousy, but uses this metaphor to help humans avoid actions that would be bad for us.

This idea that worshiping other gods or communicating with other spirits is dangerous to humans because these spirits are malicious is another component of the doctrine of "demonism" discussed in our last point, which teaches that worship of any other god and seeking communion with other types of spirits, will inevitably lead to negative consequences for humanity.

The problem is, that logic doesn't quite bear out either. There isn't any evidence that the worship of other gods or communication with other spirits is bad for humanity. In fact, for all the reasons we have discussed so far, it appears that removing the veneration of plant, animal and nature spirits, not to mention the female forms of God, from a person's theology actually do harm. It seems possible that the obsessive and unconditional focus of worship and obedience on a single God to the exclusion of all other beings and spirits might be actively harmful.

So how did this idea that God is jealous, and that many forms of worship and spiritual arts are wrong, come about?

I have a theory. This is, as far as I know, "original research"—a logical extrapolation on my part which is not directly supported by other scriptures or researchers. But it is consistent with what we know of the evolution of the monotheistic religions today, the study of comparative attitudes toward God across religions, and the study of deity behavior across religions.

There is a great deal of evidence that the God of today's monotheistic religions began life as one god from a polytheistic pantheon. Or at least, the being which started out bearing His name and being recorded in the scriptures of His people did. The God who is called Yahweh in the oldest scriptures of today's monotheistic religions bears the same name, and many of the same behaviors, as a god who originated in the Canaanite pantheon a millennia before the oldest Jewish scriptures were committed to writing.

Indeed, there are a number of Jewish and Christian academic scholars who accept that these scriptures were originally part of a polytheistic religion which splintered off of the Canaanite pantheon several thousand years ago.[5] After all, there would scarcely be reason for Biblical authors to repeatedly tell the people of Israel to stop worshiping various other gods and goddesses if such worship were not indeed common among the first people of Yahweh.[6]

One recent intriguing archaeological discovery revealed a temple dating from ancient Israel which appeared to show signs of the worship of multiple idols. While certain religious and political authorities were quick to minimize this find and characterize it as the likely center of a small polytheistic cult, others have pointed out that it was found at a location and in a strata layer which would make it a suitable candidate for *the* Temple of Solomon which was sacred to the Jews of the time period.[7]

This is important because it would explain all instances of Yahweh appearing to behave like a polytheistic god. Jealousy is an expected trait for polytheistic gods who are, indeed, finite and limited beings. So too are prohibitions on certain behaviors which might not make sense as universal rules for all humans; they may well be bestowed by a particular god on their particular devotees for purposes of cultivating specific virtues.

---

5. Smith, Mark S. (2002). (2nd ed.). Eerdmans. .

6. Meier, S.A. (1999). . In Van der Toorn, Karel; Becking, Bob; Van der Horst, Pieter Willem (eds.). Dictionary of Deities and Demons in the Bible. Eerdmans. .

7. David, A. (2021, October 27). Judahite temple by Jerusalem May Have Housed Statue of Canaanite God. Haaretz.com. https://www.haaretz.com/archaeology/2021-10-27/ty-article/judahite-temple-by-jerusalem-may-have-housed-statue-of-canaanite-god/0000017f-e2b7-d38f-a57f-e6f714c90000

Indeed, within polytheistic communities, it's common for devotees of specific gods to adhere to highly specific behavioral codes of conduct in order to cultivate the virtues of their specific god. The intention is not to suggest that the actions prohibited by these codes are always wrong for all people, but rather that people who desire to cultivate the specific virtues, and a specific relationship with this god, benefit from adhering to them.

This fits with the language of the earliest Abrahamic tests. There is within the text of Yahweh's scriptures a gradual language shift from "I am *your* god, and I have a specific covenant with you and specific rules for you" to "I am the *best* god, other gods are not only unsuitable for you specifically, but are generally inferior," to "I am the *only* God, I am responsible for everything that happens in the world and other gods literally do not exist."[8]

In this way, Yahweh's jealousy, and His rules for His people, come to be seen as statements of vice and virtue which apply to all humans and which essentially render all other religions unacceptable to the One True God. This is a unique evolution in human religious history, and arguably not a morally superior one for reasons we will discuss throughout this book.

What is interesting is that numerous traditions worldwide *do* acknowledge a sort of "God" with a capital "G." Many polytheistic religions *also* espouse the existence of a single infinite, omnipotent, and all-encompassing being which some of these religions do refer to as "God" when speaking English. However, these Gods with a capital "G" are typically quite different in character and nature from polytheistic gods. In fact, they are so different that many traditions

---

8. Gier, N. F.. Hebrew Henotheism. https://www.webpages.uid aho.edu/ngier/henotheism.htm

include both such a "God" and many lower-case "gods," since the categories are so different as to be in no way mutually exclusive.

Many people in the modern era hesitate to translate the divine One from their traditions as "God" due to the common monotheistic belief that "God" describes a being who is, among other things, jealous.

In these other traditions, the One is considered to be a being, consciousness, or living material which is all-encompassing, to underlie everything, to have created everything—but They (they are almost universally taught to encompass all genders) are not considered to have anthropomorphic characteristics common to gods, such as jealousy, demands for worship, or strong opinions about how humans should behave.

These truly infinite and complete beings are often regarded as excellent subjects for communion and contemplation for spiritual growth by the people who sense their presence, but they are generally considered to transcend the types of gods who are capable of jealousy. They are sometimes considered to have created these lesser gods specifically to assist humans through worship.

It does not seem unreasonable to speculate, then, that the monotheistic traditions of today may have been born out of a theological tradition which began worshiping a particular god, and eventually shifted to prioritizing the One who possesses many of the characteristics attributed by monotheists to their God.

This would be no shameful evolution. In fact, contemplation and communion with the One is regarded as the best way to pursue enlightenment in a number of religious systems from around the world.

Similar beings are acknowledged by enlightenment religions (in which spiritual salvation is attained through cultivation of oneness with the All, rather than through correct theological belief in a particular name of God), in a number of indigenous religions, and in

Goddess worship, which is major current within Paganism that conceptualizes all beings, including humans and gods, as having been birthed or manifested by a unified Divinity who is best-conceptualized as a mother.[9,10,11,12,13]

But if this progression were true, it would suggest a necessity to call into question the attribution of characteristics to the monotheistic God which are in conflict with the nature of a truly infinite and complete being. It would suggest that it is worth examining whether some monotheistic scriptures are truly intended to impose behavioral laws on *all* human beings, and whether all behavior displayed by the god of these first scriptures is indeed virtuous and worthy of being considered absolute moral law.

For Pagans, there is no contradiction in cultivating relationships with multiple gods, any more than there is a contradiction in cultivating relationships with multiple other living beings. It is generally acknowledged that there are many gods because there are infinite potential manifestations of divine virtue and a countless variety of

---

9. Chaudhuri, H. (1954). The Concept of Brahman in Hindu Philosophy. Philosophy East and West, 4(1), 47–66. https://doi.org/10.2307/1396951

10. Rice, Julian (1998). Before the great spirit: the many faces of Sioux spirituality. University of New Mexico Press. .

11. Maffie, J. (2015). Aztec Philosophy: Understanding a World in Motion. University Press of Colorado.

12. Laozi, & Mitchell, S. (1988). Tao Te Ching. Harper & Row, Publishers.

13. Starhawk. (1982). Dreaming the Dark: Magic, Sex, & Politics. Beacon Press.

WORLD SOUL

spiritual beings in existence who we can benefit from learning from. These gods may sometimes become jealous, just as other living beings may, but this jealousy does not suggest that it is morally wrong to speak to other gods.

For many Pagans, there is also a One Goddess, Source, Universe, or other name for the living energy and consciousness which permeates and creates all things. Different Pagan theologies have significantly different teachings about the nature and properties of this One Being, but, the frequency with which the idea of a single Divine fabric, energy, or World Soul comes up in religions across space and time is truly intriguing.

All of these traditions do seem to agree on one thing: that this infinite and unique Being does *not* experience jealousy, nor does it begrudge humans their relationships with their fellow living beings and the lesser gods who are also manifestations of the One.

As a Pagan, there is no necessity to believe in the One at all. Pagans generally become Pagan because they have had direct religious experiences with other gods or spirits who do not fit into the theologies of the monotheistic religions around them. They know that these spiritual contacts are good, nurturing, and holy, but cannot find any support for them in monotheistic congregations and may find active opposition and demonization.

But it is worth examining the ways in which concepts of the Goddess or the One found in Pagan faiths are deeply compatible with the concepts of God found in monotheistic religions. It may be that it is possible to be monotheistic in the sense of believing in one God with a big "G," one loving Creator of all beings, without discounting the existence of the many gods and spirits worshiped by one's brothers and sisters in the web of life.

And this framework may be particularly important at a time when it is becoming increasingly clear that we must become comfortable with many names and faces of God if we are to properly honor and value the divinity of all the living beings with whom we share this planet.

What Does a Theology Without These Ideas Look Like?

A theology without these ideas is simple in its essence. Most Pagan theologies share the idea that the world itself is Divine, that life is a gift from the gods, and that what is not the work of human hands must necessarily be the work of God. This view inspires a reverence for and a sense of divine kinship with all beings.

Observations of the world around us shows that humans exist in a web of ecological interdependence with our fellow species, and that humans must safeguard the existence of these fellow species if we wish to safeguard our own futures. This is not regarded merely as a scientific or practical fact, but as a religious and theological obligation in light of the belief that all living beings spring from the Divine. This is one reason why there has historically been considerable overlap between ecological activism and Pagan religious circles. It is also why many modern Pagans engage in sustainable farming or sustainable dietary choices.

The absence of a jealous God results in a radically different view of religious experiences from those found in monotheistic religions popular in the West.

Within Pagan circles, an infinite array of religious experiences can be considered legitimate divine callings which may be supported by the local community. Provided that these personal divine revelations and vocations do not actively conflict with the community's life-centered ethics, they can be assumed to be legitimate divine sendings which expand the community's knowledge of, and relationship to, the Divine.

Pagan communities tend to resemble webs of life themselves more than centralized religious organizations, with traditions and practice groups centered around different types of religious experiences and paths living in active cross-communication and frequently exchanging members as their individual spiritual growth paths progress.

Because jealousy is not considered a divine virtue, there is no conflict in working with more than one deity, or even belonging to more than one tradition at once, so long as the requirements for membership don't irreconcilably conflict. In this view, religious life is considered less the fulfillment of a set of divinely bestowed obligations and more a process of relationship which helps a person grow in performing their role to sustain the living world.

For people who are accustomed to more centralized religious organizations, this can sound chaotic. How is a person to know what the "right" thing to do is if no one God can be trusted as an absolute moral authority? How is a person to know which god they "should" worship, or what set of behavioral rules they "should" follow if many are accepted by their religious communities.

Yet as religious organizations and human authority figures prescribe narrow religious paths and increasingly fail to solve the crisis facing our world, more and more people are considering whether heavier reliance on individual judgment, rather than on centralized prescriptions, are in fact what is needed for our society's spiritual growth moving forward.

After all, what is safer? Having one moral authority who may be wrong on important matters, or encouraging each individual human to cultivate their own spirituality and moral discernment.

I invite you to come with me throughout this book as we glimpse the diverse array being cultivated in the Pagan theologies and communities of today.

Chapter Two

What is a God? The Answer May Surprise You.

Most of us in the English-speaking world are raised with monotheistic ideas around the word "God." The Christian God, for example, is the single, omnipotent, omniscient being who created everything that exists and who forbids the worship of other gods.

When you are raised with this image, there is a sort of self-reinforcing logic to it: if a God is by definition infinite and all-encompassing, for example, it doesn't make much sense for there to be more than one of them. Polytheism, then, looks like a failure of logic, and the internal contradictions inherent to the idea of a God who is both all-encompassing and jealous, both benevolent and punitive, can be more or less ignored.

But historically speaking, this image of an all-encompassing, genuinely infinite being has not been what the word "god" referred to at all.

The word we translate into English as "God" and "god" is the Greek "theos." This word, used to refer to a powerful divine intelligence, is used in the earliest Christian scriptures to refer to both the polytheistic gods of Rome and other cultures, as well as to the Christian God.[1] This is interesting because it suggests that, in some sense, in the minds of the early Christians, their God was indeed in the same category of being as these Pagan gods.

Let's look at what a "theos" was in the Greco-Roman sense. Certainly not a single, infinite being who encompasses all aspects of all beings and is responsible for all things that happen on Earth. "Theoi," plural, were beings who together *shared* power over creation, who were related but not unified, and who *between them* manifested various forms of virtue and perfection, as well as the vices that could occur as a result of imbalanced excesses of virtue.

The number of theoi were not limited, as the Greeks and Romans, like typical Pagan cultures, were happy to accept that other divine beings lived in other parts of the Earth and were even happy to adopt new deities into their pantheons if they showed an interest in being adopted. Some Greco-Roman gods are known to have been explicitly adopted from other cultures out of a desire to gain the virtues or favors that came with worshiping that deity.

This has been the norm throughout human history. The practice of acknowledging, revering, and communing with a host of divine enti-

---

1. Stewart, D.. What does the Greek term Theos (god) mean?. Blue Letter Bible. https://www.blueletterbible.org/faq/don_stewart/don_stewart_1306.cfm

ties has been found on every continent, as has the practice of respecting and sometimes adopting the deities of other cultures. Humans have typically cultivated relationships with their own divine allies, and demonized each others' only when war or political conflict gave them economic reasons to do so.

Now, as mentioned, many cultures *have* espoused belief in a single creative energy, consciousness, or world soul which creates and manifests all things. This unifying life force has been called by many names across every populated continent—none of which translate into English very well, because the closest translation is "God," but God in the sense it is most frequently used also implies personality traits and opinions which this One energy simply does not have.

When Hindus speak of "God" in English, they are typically referring to Brahman, which is their word for the world soul, the true creator and manifester of all things, the God by any other name of their theology. Yet this God does not preclude the existence of countless gods in the sense of "theoi." In fact, in many strains of Hinduism, Brahman does not demand to be worshiped directly but instead creates and manifests countless gods in the same way It creates and manifests countless people.[2]

This is what some Hindus mean when they say that Hinduism is at once monotheistic and polytheistic. While this may seem like a contradiction, it is actually a reflection of the limitations of the English language, which refers to the One who creates and manifests all things using the same word, "God" or "theos," as the separate concept of a host of divine yet limited gods and goddesses.

The fact that English has no equivalent word to the Hindu Brahman, the Nahua Teotl, the Chinese Tao, the Lakota Wakan Tanka,

---

2. Jeaneane D. Fowler (2002). . Sussex Academic Press. p. 330. .

the Yoruba Olodumare, etc. has muddied theological discussions for centuries by misleadingly referring to radically different beings and concepts using the same word "God" or "gods."

There are entire volumes that can be written about what we can each learn about our own theology by studying the nature attributed to God and gods by different cultures. Today we are here, first and foremost, to understand how Pagans think about God and gods differently from other religions that are currently popular in the West, and why these differences are beneficial to Paganism's ability to address our world's humanitarian and environmental crises.

So what are the benefits of polytheistic theologies which postulate the existence of more than one god?

Benefits of Polytheism

Pagan theologians have characterized monotheism as "religious imperialism," as it can elevate to the status of theology the idea that there is only one "correct" culture or way of being.[3] While this may be a slight oversimplification, this statement is a good starting place to understand why polytheistic religious systems, or at least religious systems which *look* polytheistic, might be more protected from religious abuses and theological mistakes than monotheistic ones.

One traditional monotheistic argument has been that a religious system with many gods, none of whom are considered to be absolute moral authorities, must be morally confusing. It is not uncommon in my work to encounter monotheists who ask how Pagans can possibly have a sense of right and wrong if they don't have a single God or holy book to listen to on this count.

---

3. Adler, M. (1979). Drawing Down the Moon. Penguin Group.

We will discuss the answer to this question in much more satisfying detail in Chapter 5, but for now I would like to turn this question on its head: what are the dangers of assuming that a single deity is an absolute and infallible moral authority?

Arguably, the dangers are great. Bloody wars between city-states have been motivated by conflicts between polytheistic gods; global wars featuring physical and cultural genocide have been waged by empires claiming to have a sacred duty to spread the One True Religion around the world.

The attitude found in many monotheistic religions of today is that proper worship of the One True God requires the total submission of one's free will, judgment, and ultimately one's life to this One True God. Everything that this God or His emissaries say must be taken as absolute moral law, and a person who experiences doubt or the impulse to disobey is considered to be guilty of selfishness and lack of faith. Because all matters of feeling, thought, and action are potential grounds for disobedience to such a God, all such matters become subject to both self-policing and community policing.

Boundaries are not respected and may even be considered sinful or unhealthy by such Gods and their human emissaries. A person's consent is often considered morally unimportant compared to the absolute moral rightness of such a God's will. It doesn't matter if something feels morally wrong to you: if God or the person you believe to be his emissary says it is right, it must be right.

People who point out that these attributes common to monotheism are hallmarks of an abusive relationship are told that this would be true—if the relationship partner were human. But because the relationship partner is the infinite and infinitely loving God, we must submit our own wills and lives completely to Him if we want to obtain a positive outcome in this life or the next.

The more enlightened parties among monotheistic religious leaders will deny this description. Indeed, strains of monotheism exist which recognize the importance of boundaries and consent. But in order to do so, they must teach these ideas essentially as exceptions to the norms preached within their religion. True virtue lies in submitting oneself totally to God and His will; *but* boundaries are important in human relationships. Moral righteousness is determined by God's will, not by the consent of living beings; *but* consent is important in human relationships.

Now, what if there were no "buts?" What if one's theology had boundaries, consent, and an imperative to exercise one's individual moral judgment baked into the fabric of divine relationships in the same way that absolute submission is baked into the fabric of monotheism? What if boundaries, consent, and individual moral discernment were considered to be the starting point for all relationships between living beings?

This is what polytheism offers.

The same attributes of polytheism which make it "confusing" or "chaotic" in the eyes of those accustomed to a more authoritarian approach allow it to incorporate protocols and values of respect between all living beings. It does this precisely by dividing divine authority between multiple individual deities, and in the process demands the constant exercise of moral judgment by individuals.

In modern Pagan communities, deities are generally considered to be bound by the same best practices concerning boundaries and consent as humans are. This is possible, and indeed *required* because of the existence of multiple gods who are all understood to be capable of both vice and virtue.

Because the idea that "if a god does it, it must be morally right" does not exist in polytheistic religions, virtue is found not in unconditional obedience to a god or a human religious authority, but in the healthy and respectful navigation of relationships with divine beings whose judgment cannot be assumed to be universal or flawless.

In fact, some Pagans report that their deities will make unreasonable requests of them specifically to test their ability and willingness to exercise good boundaries and moral judgment. This is not possible in a system where it is assumed that one God is unconditionally in the moral right, and that any limitation on one's obedience to Him constitutes a sin.

Healthy relationships between humans and deities are held to the same standards as healthy relationships between humans and other humans, and in the process healthy relationship standards and skills are baked into religious practice instead of being in *conflict* with religious practice.

This in turn helps to encourage healthy relationship practices between humans within Pagan communities. When the procedures and standards used to speak with gods are the same as the procedures and standards used to speak with friends, family, colleagues, and potential romantic partners, it is easy to cultivate a higher standard of respect for all beings.

This also translates into a basis for moral judgements which are more responsive to new information and changing conditions than the top-down centralized method of religious law.

How many discussions have been had about whether old religious laws need to be changed or updated in the face of new material conditions, ethical understandings, or scientific information? How many discussions have been had about whether it is sinful to refuse to enforce religious laws and punishments that seem cruel and barbaric under current circumstances?

These discussions are much easier when they take place in a polytheistic context where it is generally acknowledged that different deities have different ideas about how humans should behave, and that boundaries and consent are a proper part of the human-deity relationship.

Some followers of Pagan gods *do* choose to be bound by strict behavioral codes and punishments which may seem cruel if enforced on unconsenting people, but which constitute tools for the development of virtue when chosen freely by consenting devotees.

The inappropriateness of enforcing religious law on unconsenting people takes on a whole new dimension in a theology in which different peoples have different gods, who probably have different codes of behavior for them. In Paganism, coercive evangelism is not just a human rights violation; it is a violation of the deities who are already in relationship with the people who are being evangelized.

Monotheism too often facilitates imperialism, colonialism, and ultimately genocide by suggesting that there is only one "right" way to do things and that all other ways of being should be wiped out. Polytheism does not even allow this mindset, since it requires acknowledging the existence of multiple divine authorities and multiple divinely ordered ways of being.

To navigate this milieu of thousands of gods and thousands of behavioral codes, Pagans are encouraged to listen to their own divine spark, their own divine callings, and to exercise best practices around boundaries, consent, and moral judgment.

For all of these reasons, a growing number of people are taking renewed interest in the Pagan and polytheistic worldviews which accommodate the deities they have seen in their own divine visions. And there is reason to believe that the protocols being developed by these communities may equip their members to resolve human rights and environmental crises better than the monotheistic tradition of obedience to established authorities.

A Few Last Notes About Gods

One distinction that ought to be discussed here is the distinction between "hard" and "soft" polytheism. This distinction has been a source of much contention within Pagan communities, and I believe some of this contention is unnecessary.

In hard polytheism, many gods are believed to have literal, separate, independent existences, in just the same way that individual humans are separate from each other. In this view all gods are in some sense finite, since it is impossible for so many beings to all be infinite without being coexistent. Hard polytheists tend to emphasize respect for individual deities, traditions, and cultures, as they do not believe that all deities are ultimately the same deity or that all forms of worship are ultimately acceptable to all deities.

In "soft" polytheism, on the other hand, different gods may be thought of as manifestations or faces of the single, unified creator of the universe. This view is common in Goddess monotheism, where different goddesses from different cultures may sometimes be treated as different "faces" of the same Goddess. Soft polytheists often emphasize similarities between different religions and pantheons, seeking to draw parallels between them and in this way expand their understanding of what they may ultimately believe to be a single universal deity.

Interestingly, it could be argued that theologies like some Hindu theologies are *both* hard and soft polytheism. These theologies teach that all gods *are* manifestations or faces of the one Brahman—but also that the gods are just as unconscious of this fact as humans are of their own nature as manifestations of Brahman, and therefore behave and deserve to be treated as separate and distinct individuals.

Gods and Angels: Things to Know

You may notice that the concept of "gods" as I describe them here are similar to the Abrahamic concept of angels. Angels in the Abrahamic traditions are considered to be powerful divine entities which are wildly diverse in form and character, and which are created by the infinite and all-encompassing God to fulfill different roles in creation.

Pagan and Abrahamic theologians alike have pointed out that conflicts between these two theologies could be resolved simply by considering gods as angels.[4] This is an intriguing suggestion, but there is a problem with it that we must address. In Abrahamic theology, traditionally, angels have no free will and no capacity for creativity.

Going back to Jewish theology, angels are specifically believed *not* to possess that part of "God's own image and likeness" which permits free will and creativity. They are strictly servants and messengers, incapable of behaving like Pagan gods in the senses of creating new beings and acting under their own agency for their own reasons.

Christianity has continued this tradition, teaching that it is the ability of Pagan gods to act of their own volition instead of being restricted to following God's orders which makes them dangerous and evil. Per Christian teachings, beings who possess their own agency and free will are inherently untrustworthy.

Interestingly, Islam does acknowledge the existence of a class of spiritual beings who have their own free will and agency. These are

---

4. DiZerega, G. (2005). Pagans & Christians: The Personal Spiritual Experience. Llewellyn Publications.

the djinn, who are considered to be created spiritual beings similar to humans in their capacity for either obedience or disobedience to God. Islam does not take as bleak a view of djinn as Christianity takes of Pagan gods, teaching that djinn can be faithful followers of God just like humans. But it does generally forbid intentionally initiating communication with djinn, much less collaborating, communing with, or worshiping them.

It is possible that a time may come for monotheists to reconsider their belief that only spiritual beings which lack free will can be trusted. A theology which accepts that the One may have Its own reasons to create many gods would do a great deal for peace and understanding between monotheistic and polytheistic religions.

Chapter Three

On the Sacredness of Life

All religions share a fairly strong opinion that life is sacred. Prohibitions against killing and teachings about the beauty of the divine gift that is the living world feature prominently in every religion I am aware of. Because living beings are considered to be sacred, religious laws about treating other beings with kindness and compassion are often considered to be supreme laws in religions around the world.

If it were that simple, we would be dealing with fewer humanitarian atrocities and environmental crises today. If humans were universally regarded as children of God who may never be harmed under religious law, and other living beings were similarly regarded, our grandchildren would be inheriting a better world. This is such a simple concept that I do not feel the need to explain it in excruciating detail. Everyone of every religion knows what it is to look at another living being and see God inside of them.

But as it is, many religions have exemptions or contradictions to this allegedly supreme law, and these must be critically discussed if our religious communities are to make real progress against the abuses and destruction we have so far failed to act against. Claiming that the moral failures of our communities and societies are down to individual sinfulness, *not* theological flaws, has not been solving the problem.

We must seriously consider whether the way our religions are being taught is promoting or enabling the ongoing destruction, and what changes must be made to change the tide. We have no choice but to change the tide of destruction, and we cannot honestly tell ourselves that we have done everything in our power to do so until we have performed this painful task of examining our own theologies for potential roots of evil.

These exceptions and "guardrails" on taking the sacredness of life "too far" fall into three general categories:

1. Part of the purpose of life is to fight and die in battle. Common in the ancient world but far less common today, this has been the most common exception to sacredness of life teachings in Pagan faiths. While not precisely contradicting the sacredness and goodness of life, this teaching *does* suggest that *part* of a sacred life is killing and dying. Often justified by observations of the natural world which show animals dying and killing as part of their survival strategies, this exception is most commonly interpreted by Pagans today as an exhortation to be willing to fight and die in defense of the defenseless if it should become necessary rather than as an exhortation to seek out wars to fight in. Indeed, many modern Pagan communities have specifically updated the warrior ethos of their heritage to specify that the virtues of courage and self-sacrifice should be used in fights for freedom, justice, and environmental conservation rather than in nationalistic

warfare. Some have explicitly declared violators of human rights to be their enemies for religious purposes.

2. There are categories of beings who exist only to serve or be sacrificed for others. When a theology teaches that the very purpose of a being's existence is to be used and/or killed according to the wishes of another, horrifying abuses can be justified as part of a religious order. I would argue that variations on this theme include some Christian teachings about humanity's dominion over the natural world, some variations on the old Christian doctrine of Divine Right, which taught that a ruler's subjects were made to serve, fight for, and die for their rulers, and some teachings about caste and class around the world in which certain categories of people have been considered to be unworthy of compassion or to be recipients of divine punishment.

3. The material world is so corrupt and flawed that it is sometimes desirable to inflict cruelty and even death in this life in an attempt to save a soul from a torturous afterlife. This teaching is on its most graphic display in the old Christian idea of "punishing the body to save the soul," which played a major role in the systematic torture and genocide of many indigenous and heretical religious groups. These cruelties were justified by claiming to save those who underwent forced conversions from the fires of Hell while protecting the living from the soul-destroying ideologies espoused by devil worshipers and heretics. Fortunately this idea is now considered almost universally unacceptable by modern Christian groups, but concerningly, writings which express and condone this idea can be found among the writings of

theologians who are still considered founding members of modern Christian sects. This raises the specter that, unless official statements are made condemning and removing these teachings, this idea could resurge if material or political conditions change sufficiently.

4. The idea that the living world is a test, not a place to be happy. This idea holds that the world is designed solely as a test of one's moral fiber prior to an eternal afterlife, and that for this reason, it is futile or even morally wrong to try to make this life a better place.

This idea is popular in some strains of both Christianity and Islam, though religions which teach reincarnation can also fall prey to arguing that those who suffer must be assigned to suffer due to karmic sins in past lives. In some theologies, it has been argued that "making the test easier" by improving material conditions on this Earth actually does a disservice to living beings who can only expect to experience eternal happiness if they pass the test that has been divinely assigned to them in this life. Needless to say, this interpretation has historically been popular with religious, political, and economic leaders who seek to justify cruel and destructive practices and to demonize activists and rebels who seek to make the world a better place. The idea that improving living conditions on this Earth is somehow a sign of moral weakness or a failure of faith in the afterlife is still expressed by some Christian and Muslim writers today.

It's easy to see how all of these ideas could impede the creation of a better world. Items 2-4 can be used to actively demonize people who seek to improve and prevent humanitarian crises if the humanitarian crises are argued to be divinely ordained.

While it is difficult to understand why anyone would espouse such ideas given the near-universal agreement among humans that helping people is good and allowing them to suffer is bad, we do still occasionally find religious leaders who argue that *some* types of suffering and death are good because God wills them.

Even in the 21st century we have seen some Christian leaders claim that certain disease epidemics or natural disasters were God's punishment of sinners who have angered God by demanding too many rights and freedoms,[1] and a number of self-identified Christian and Muslim leaders claim that doing God's will requires rolling back human rights.

Some theologians of both religions have argued to me in private conversations that since life on this Earth is designed as a test, not a final destination, human happiness on this Earth should not be considered important in the interpretation of religious law.

So how do we fight these ideas which are still found in the archives of some of this world's most popular religions? How do we ensure that any anticipation we may have of our afterlife does not cause us to neglect or harm our fellow living beings in this life? How do we ensure that the law of love does remain supreme, even if some theologians may argue that it does not deserve to be at the top of the list of commandments?

This starts with a personal resolution. We must each look into our hearts and ask what we believe to be the most important moral law.

If our answer is that compassion and empathy are the highest moral laws, we can safely take any actions necessary to ensure that these are also the moral laws prioritized by our religious communities.

---

1. Cable News Network. (2010, January 13). Pat Robertson says Haiti paying for "pact to the devil." CNN. http://www.cnn.com/2010/US/01/13/haiti.pat.robertson/index.html

If we find that we feel there are higher goods than empathy or compassion for living beings, or that we feel it risky to prioritize these virtues too much, this bears further self-examination. What are the logical consequences of the impulses in our hearts? Do these logical consequences create a world we would like our children to live in?

Now that we have taken a look at the *exceptions* to the nearly universal impulse to consider all life sacred, let's take a look at how modern Pagan communities are teaching and practicing this value as supreme, and what we can learn from them.

Paganism Teaches that Life on Earth is Fundamentally Good

Pagan theologies generally lack teachings that life on this Earth is not important, or cannot be made good. In the absence of teachings about the material world being "fallen" or "corrupted," the vast majority of Pagan traditions instead teach that the material world is "transparent to transcendence." The idea that all living beings are divine in origin, and all have the potential to be divine messengers or teachers, is nearly universal among Pagan traditions.

The teaching found in many Pagan traditions that humans and other living beings are all divine creations, and perhaps even manifestations of divine purpose, creates religious communities which are person-centered in a way that is not always found in other religious traditions.

Instead of treating a religious community primarily as a means to the end of honoring the gods, modern Pagan religious communities often view their purpose as being the support of members in manifesting their individual divine purposes. This often translates to an emphasis on healing and supporting community members, where the goal is not merely to rehabilitate them to be more effective servants of the gods, but where supporting each other is considered an end unto itself.

Under these value arrangements, deities are often seen as allies in the task of healing individuals and the material world, rather than individuals and the material world being seen as tools toward the end of serving or glorifying the gods. If all living beings are sacred, then it makes sense for relationships between humanity and the gods to be reciprocal instead of one-sided.

Reciprocal relationships are a frequent topic of discussion in Pagan circles. It is not just reciprocity between gods and humans that is required for a healthy web of life, but also reciprocity between humans and other species. Many indigenous religions and revived Pagan traditions include explicit teachings about the duty of humanity to keep its important partner species alive and healthy if humanity itself wishes to remain alive and healthy.

The impact of these priorities on Pagan religious laws and practices is profound. In modern Pagan communities there tends to be an almost complete lack of attention to policing individuals' sex lives and spiritual practices, for example, except in instances where these become so dysfunctional as to cause harm to individuals in the community. Concern about idolatry is nonexistent in Pagan circles, as is concern about sexual activities which are consensual on the part of all involved.

Instead, Pagan religious laws and sermons are more likely to pertain to topics like how to live in ways that do not damage our partner species, how to effectively respect and support each other, and how to effectively respect and support ourselves.

Modern Pagan leaders have found that that last topic needs a shocking amount of attention. Between a capitalist culture which shames and blames those who struggle with poverty in too many parts of the world and the commonality of theologies which shame and blame people over victimless "sins," my experience has been that Pagans and modern people in general often have more difficulty treating themselves with respect and dignity than treating other people in the same way.

Many people come to Pagan congregations very prepared to extend grace, empathy, and support to others—but totally unprepared to extend these same quantities to themselves. This service-oriented selflessness can actually impair an individual's ability to make the world a better place by causing them to doubt their sense of right and wrong and preventing them from accruing the necessary resources it takes to make a difference in the world.

This is the goal and the logical conclusion of the economic motivations we will discuss in Chapter 7, and it is difficult to address in religious communities which sometimes treat individuals only as flawed servants of a judgemental God. In a theology that prioritizes the welfare of mortal living beings over the services of divine beings—the gods, after all, hardly *need* our help, while our fellow mortal beings do—it becomes easier for community life and ritual to turn to the healing of a worshiper's own wounds.

A major focus of my own Pagan work is helping individuals to heal fully so that they can become more powerful agents of positive change. It is interesting to me that I have seen relatively little attention to this pursuit in other religious communities I have visited, where pastoral care is generally available, but the main focus of religious community life is on executing worship activities rather than on empowering community members.

This is just one powerful example of how a theology which prioritizes the sacredness of biological living beings, rather than obedience to a transcendent God or the attainment of paradise in the next life, can be more well-equipped to make this world a better place than religions which prioritize these realities which can sometimes seem far distant from the living beings who are now suffering on Earth.

There is one more set of religious teachings we must confront and question in our task of discovering why the religious communities which are dominant on Earth today have failed to prevent our current catastrophes.

If you were uncomfortable with what I described here about person-centered religious communities, examine your reactions as you read this next section. Are the ideas contained here informing your instincts? Are they the reason you are uncomfortable with the idea of putting "too much" emphasis on the healing and welfare of mortal beings?

If you have such discomfort how is it affecting your work in the fight for the safety, freedom, and dignity of all people?

Pagan Religions Don't Give Central Importance to Sin and Punishment

One major difference between Pagan theologies and monotheistic theologies is the way these theologies think about ethics, morality, and sin. In monotheistic theologies, "sin" is when a human being does something that is contrary to God's will. In Paganism, this definition doesn't make sense since there are multiple gods who can have conflicting wills, none of which are considered absolute moral authorities.

This is an extremely important distinction because of how right and wrong are defined in each system. In a monotheistic distinction, where God's will is the be-all and end-all of morality, questions like the harm and good of living creatures do not necessarily come into the moral equation. Something is right if God says so, even if it does harm; something is wrong if God says so, even if it does good.

This is why some monotheistic theologians have been known to openly argue that harms and goods done to living creatures are ultimately morally unimportant. In the words of some Christian and Muslim theologians, helping our fellow beings is sometimes right because God said so; but harming our fellow living beings is *not* wrong if God ordered us to do so, or if God inflicted the harm himself. In fact, it may be morally wrong to *refuse* to harm our fellow beings if God has commanded us to do so.

This same logic underlies the confusion and discomfort about consent culture in some religious circles. Theologians of some religions have consistently expressed that the rightness or wrongness of a sexual relationship is determined by whether it conforms to religious law in terms of gender combination and the proper sealing of marriage vows by a person of the clergy.

Some Christian theologians I have spoken to have seemed genuinely confused about how sexual behavior could be morally right if it does not meet these requirements, or how it could be morally wrong if it does. They seemed not to believe that coercive marriages or marital rape were real problems, or that sexual relationships which did not meet their cultures' criteria for marriage could be beneficial under any circumstances.

The idea that the consent or lack thereof of an individual human could have any real importance in determining the rightness or wrongness of an action was alien to them. As far as they were concerned, it was the meeting of external God-given guidelines which made an activity right or wrong, not the consent of the people involved.

This becomes additionally problematic when religious leaders become preoccupied with punishing victimless "sins" like unsanctioned (but consensual) sexual activity, heresy, or the practice of forbidden spiritual arts. These "sins" generally do not cause harm to living beings, but in some theologies, they are the major focus of corrective action by God, religious leaders, and religious communities.

This is unfortunate, because these corrective actions can not only *create* harm to living beings where none existed before, but can sap virtually all of a religious community's attention which could otherwise be devoted to preventing and reversing harms done by humanitarian crises and climate change.

This is one reason why "religion" has a bad reputation in too many communities. Those who have been exposed to religious communities which are highly punitive and preoccupied with victimless "sins" can easily reach the conclusion that the entire purpose of religion is to divert attention from the real harms being done in the world and focus attention on curtailing individual sexual and religious freedom instead.

I will confess that I briefly espoused this idea after a bad breakup with a church that was more interested in punishing sexual "sins" than in offering any assistance at all to youth who were in acute mental and spiritual distress. Many other Pagans and atheists I've spoken to have reported the same thing; when one's major exposure to religion is to theologies which actively demonize environmentalism and human rights progress, it is no wonder that one might form the opinion that *all* religion is designed to curtail freedom and limit respect for life.

Fortunately, I discovered that theologies do exist which put the welfare of living beings first, and that indeed, these have been the norm more often than not throughout human history. But the idea of religion as an inherently life-affirming and life-valuing force was almost alien to me after spending years in a religion whose theology seemed almost completely indifferent to human suffering and whose leaders actively demonized those who sought to expand the rights of living beings.

Unfortunately, enough theologies still focus more intently on punishing "sin" than on providing for the welfare of living beings that a theological focus on sin and punishment continues to be a major impediment to solving the humanitarian and environmental crises of today.

One common feature of sin-and-punishment oriented theologies is the claim that violent crimes and victimless "sins" all arise from the same source: disobedience to God. They then argue that the way to prevent violence is to strictly punish *all* sin, since the same impulses which lead to unauthorized sexual activity, heresy, and the practice of forbidden spiritual arts are those which also lead to violence.

This teaching might be alright if it were true, but it's not. In fact, studies across areas ranging from criminal justice to child discipline to cultural models of shame and guilt suggest that more severe punishments can actually increase the risk that the person being punished will do violence in the future.[2,3] Several theories have been proposed to explain why this may be.

---

2. Gershoff ET. Corporal punishment by parents and associated child behaviors and experiences: a meta-analytic and theoretical review. Psychological Bulletin. 2002;128(4):539-579.

3. Sussex Publishers. (n.d.). Why punishment doesn't reduce crime. Psychology Today. https://www.psychologytoday.com/us/blog/crime-and-punishment/201804/why-punishment-doesnt-reduce-crime

One theory is that the use of physical and emotional violence as punishment instills in children the idea that these forms of violence are the normal means by which righteous authority is expressed. Such children may go on to use similarly violent tactics to assert their own authority and righteousness when they find themselves confronted with behavior they don't like from others later in life.[4,5]

Another theory suggests that traumatizing punishments cause dysregulation of the nervous system, making it harder for people to control their emotional reactions in the future. Clinical evidence does suggest that people who are subjected to extreme pain, fear, or shame often find it more difficult to regulate their emotional responses in the future, and may be more likely to lash out at those they feel threatened or wronged by.[6,7]

---

4. Gilligan, J. (2003). Shame, Guilt, and Violence. Social Research, 70(4), 1149–1180. http://www.jstor.org/stable/40971965

5. Amy Morin, L. (2022, November 9). Surprising facts about spanking and corporal punishment. Verywell Family. https://www.verywellfamily.com/facts-about-corporal-punishment-1094806#:~:text=Corporal%20punishment%20models%20aggressive%20behavior,having%20power%20over%20someone%20else.

6. Lori Korthals, M. S. (2017, February 2). A look at corporal punishment. Science of Parenting. https://blogs.extension.iastate.edu/scienceofparenting/2017/02/02/a-look-at-corporal-punishment/

7. Jacob Nordman, Xiaoyu Ma, Qinhua Gu, Michael Potegal, He Li, Alexxai V. Kravitz, Zheng Li. Potentiation of divergent medial amygdala pathways drives experience-dependent aggression escalation. The Journal of Neuroscience, 2020; JN-RM-0370-20 DOI:

Clearly, then, the hypothesis that harsh punishment of all violations of religious law will keep violence at bay is flawed. It seems more likely, in light of recent research, that this philosophy will actually *increase* violence in society and in the global community.

This is seen as a big problem by some religious leaders, who consider their right to punish people for breaking religious taboos integral to their religious freedom. Interestingly, some Pagans would agree with this assessment—provided that the punisher and punishee have both consented to live by the rules and endure the punishment.

Unfortunately, consent often does not figure into the calculations of religious leaders who argue that they should be allowed to punish *all* people in their societies or all people in the world, who break their religious laws.

Some readers might suggest that I am making too big a deal out of this matter of sin and punishment. After all, how often do we hear someone seriously proposing that people who have sex before marriage be publicly flogged or stoned to death?

Well, more often than you might think, actually. Unintended pregnancy remains a major threat to the lives of women in many parts of the world, not just because of the medical risks, but because violent retaliation may occur from their societies or from their own families if they are discovered to have engaged in sex before marriage.

This is a major concern of emergency medicine physicians, even in the U.S., where legal policies allowing minors to obtain birth control and abortion without their parents' consent are designed in part to protect girls from physical violence they may suffer at the hands of their own families if they are discovered to be pregnant.

According to research, one in three American teens who choose not to tell their families they are pregnant have a fear of physical violence if their families discover they have been sexually active.[8] Public health scientists have similar fears about new laws that have been introduced in some U.S. states requiring schools to inform families if their children display homosexual or trans gendered behaviors.

I would argue that these outbursts of punitive violence exist among followers of some theologies because some of these theologies are so completely oriented around sin and punishment. These are major themes in the Bible and the Qur'an; where the right of God to punish sinners and the obligation of God's faithful to do the same are repeatedly emphasized.

While Christianity is sometimes practiced as a religion of forgiveness and God's unconditional love, the necessity for forgiveness arises in the first place because of an underlying assumption that God is morally entitled to punish humans for our various failings with eternal torment. It is not difficult to see, then, why devotees of such theologies may feel morally offended, or even feel that their freedom of religion is threatened, if their right to violently punish sinners is taken away.

This, obviously, does not help with the resolution of humanitarian crises. Especially when these crises involve the suffering of "sinners" such as women who have been sexually active before marriage, LGBTQ people, or people who refuse to convert to the "right" religion. When ecological activists can also be painted as "sinners" who

---

8. Claire McCarthy, M. (2017, January 24). Why medical experts say that teens should be allowed to make the abortion decision without telling their parents. Harvard Health. https://www.health.harvard.edu/blog/why-medical-experts-say-that-teens-should-be-allowed-to-make-the-abortion-decision-without-telling-their-parents-2017012411079

need to be punished and cast out of society because of their "idolatrous" love of the natural world, we have a real problem.

How many of these teachings are found in your religion? How often do you see people who are struggling with violent impulses because they are angry at someone for refusing to follow the rules of their religion? I unfortunately see and speak to people in this situation on a regular basis. This is what tells me that many religions must change their theology if they truly wish to extinguish any support for violence among their ranks.

I have spent several pages now complaining about the effects of punitive theologies; how are Pagans different in this respect?

As I have mentioned above, Pagans simply lack the idea that the human relationship with God centers on sin and punishment. It is possible to commit harm in Paganism, and it is possible to displease the gods. But displeasing a god is not automatically considered to be a moral wrong, or grounds for violent punishment. The seeking of forgiveness for punishable offenses is certainly not understood to be the basis of all human relationships with the gods.

In fact, gods who demand violent punishment of those who displease them are generally not well-loved in Pagan communities. In communities where *all* relationships are based on healthy understandings of boundaries and consent, even gods must play by the rules if they wish to be included. Pagans rarely hear their gods demand violence today, perhaps because any god who did would be rapidly removed from the altar in most modern Pagan communities.

Sin and punishment simply are not central to Pagan understandings of the relationship between humanity and the divine. In fact, the topic of divine punishment only comes up when discussing harms a human may have done to their fellow living beings.

Most Pagan communities do believe that divine punishment is possible and potentially justified in these cases, but see this more as a matter of violence in defense of the defenseless than as a matter of punishment for not following the rules. The only situations in which most Pagans consider it morally acceptable for a god to punish someone are those in which the target of the punishment has consistently and willfully harmed others.

Such unfortunate situations are generally not the focus of congregational contemplation or action; instead, spiritual healing and cultivating relationships with nature spirits and deities who are more interested in empowering humanity to be better than in punishing us for our sins are the focus of most Pagan religious activities.

The Pagan policy of honoring living beings above all else has created a situation where compassion and empathy are the primary yardstick for morality. In the absence of teachings that obedience to God must take priority over these yardsticks, it has been easy for Pagan congregations to shift their attention to humanitarian and environmental crises without feeling that they are abandoning the traditional focus of their religion.

As this chapter draws to a close, I invite you to consider ways in which teachings about sin and punishment might be making human rights issues worse within your community. Do you deal with community members who express hatred or violent sentiments toward people they perceive as sinners? Is there a way you can bring this conversation to your congregation and consider what your God really wants from you as a community?

Are the sacredness of living beings and the Law of Love truly at the top of the priority list in your religious community? If not, do you want to put them there? Why or why not? What theological reasons do you have for prioritizing or de-prioritizing the welfare of living beings as a focus of your religious activities?

If the law of love needs to be restored to its place of supremacy in your religion, how might you start working to accomplish that?

We will now examine the world-changing potential of extending this reverence for living beings beyond the human species.

Chapter Four

The Web of Life, the Divine Family

We have discussed the fact that Pagan religions often do not consider humanity to be uniquely theologically privileged among living beings. In a world which is divine and inhabited by gods and spirits, humans cannot always assume themselves to be in the absolute moral right. This has been a feature of indigenous religions and reincarnation religions, perhaps since humanity first came into existence.

But mainstream Christianity and the prevailing economic philosophies of recent decades in the East and West alike have treated serious consideration for the rights of non-human beings as a dangerous heresy. Most of the Pagans I spoke to in writing this book reported having been treated by Christians as ignorant at best, wicked and heretical at worst, when they expressed concerns for the souls or treatment of animals or over the destruction of beloved nature areas as children.

Descriptions of this hostility may seem overblown, but they had made a major impact on every Pagan I spoke to. Many had their most profound religious experiences when communing with nature, only to be told that these experiences were suspicious or that their church's theology had no room for them. Many became alarmed as children by adults' seeming indifference to the welfare of plant and animal life and their sometimes hostile responses to questions about them. Young people who were upset about the destruction of beloved fields and forests to build houses and strip malls were more often treated as complaining children than as budding activists in Christian America.

Nor is Christianity the only culprit here: non-religious followers of both capitalism and communism have behaved similarly while overseeing the clear-cutting of forests and the factory farming of animals, even going to far as to ban or censor books and scientific reports which they worried may turn public opinion against these cruel and dangerous activities. Communist China has famously classified many animistic religious practices and works of environmentalist literature among its banned "outdated and oppressive beliefs" since the beginning of its rapid industrialization,[1][2] and capitalist America has seen

---

1. Liu X. Shamanic Culture's Reconnection of Earth and Heaven (Xu Ditiantong) in the New Era in China: The Dialectical Relationship between Material Civilization and Cultural Intimacy. Religions. 2023; 14(4):500. https://doi.org/10.3390/rel14040500

2. Hao Tan. (2023, July 31). China's "Silent spring" has many more political hurdles to jump. The Conversation. https://theconversation.com/chinas-silent-spring-has-many-more-political-hurdles-to-jump-38604

Christian leaders back politicians in censoring climate science[3,4] and arguing that environmentalism is an immoral threat to Christianity and to the American way of life.[5,6]

Anyone who has spent a significant amount of time with non-human living beings can sense deep commonalities between ourselves and them. Science has now begun to confirm what stewards of plant and animal life have known for many years: that non-human beings engage in far more communication and information processing than Western science had once assumed. Using chemical messages, plants, animals, and microbes "speak" to us in meaningful ways, and their

---

3. Burnett, J. (2011, October 27). Scientists say Texas Agency edits out climate change. NPR. https://www.npr.org/2011/10/27/141748024/scientists-say-texas-agency-edits-out-climate-change

4. Waldman, S. (2018, January 10). Climate web pages erased and obscured under trump. Scientific American. https://www.scientificamerican.com/article/climate-web-pages-erased-and-obscured-under-trump/

5. Bob Allen, Managing editor at EthicsDaily.com from 2003-2009. (2019, February 28). Falwell says global warming tool of satan. Good Faith Media. https://goodfaithmedia.org/falwell-says-global-warming-tool-of-satan-cms-8596/

6. Barone, E. (2022, November 18). Christians have conflicting views on climate change: Poll. Time. https://time.com/6234932/climate-change-religion-survey/

internal chemical processes respond to the environment in ways that look much more like conscious experience than was once assumed.[7]

This should not surprise us. After all, we know that all life on Earth is closely biologically related. Evidence from genetic and biochemical analyses show that all life on Earth is descended from a common ancestor. All are descended from a single living being. The results of these analyses lend a surprisingly literal truth to the teaching espoused by many historic religions that all living beings are divine siblings by virtue of having been created together and sustained together by the same divine forces.

The idea that we can experience spiritual fulfillment from the company of our divine kin in the plant and animal kingdoms is now also thoroughly proven. Countless studies have shown that spending time with animals and living in the presence of plants significantly alleviates mental illness in many people and leads to elevated mood, improved self-care, and decreased incidents of violent behavior.

The mechanisms for these changes are still not fully understood, and are hypothesized to have something to do with how our brains are designed and how our bodies experience nonverbal communications with our fellow species. But the effects are proven thoroughly enough that a number of experts recommend programs designed around the

---

7. Lawrence, N. (2022, August 25). The radical new experiments that hint at plant consciousness. New Scientist. https://www.newscientist.com/article/mg25534012-800-the-radical-new-experiments-that-hint-at-plant-consciousness/

use of contact with animals and plants to treat illness and prevent crime.[8,9,10,11]

An animist would say that we are more human in the presence of our divine kin because humanity is not designed to live alone. They would say that we can no more experience the fullness of humanity in isolation from our divine siblings than a polar bear can behave naturally in a zoo or a cow can behave naturally in a factory farming stall. None of us are made to live in isolation from our divine kin, and we all suffer when we are made to do so.

These are all empirical, physical facts. We now know that at a biochemical level, we are closely related to other species and appear to suffer acute mental and physical problems when we are not allowed to live in community with them. Some might argue that these are

---

8. Troy, A., Morgan Grove, J., & O'Neil-Dunne, J. (2012). The relationship between tree canopy and crime rates across an urban–rural gradient in the Greater Baltimore region. Landscape and Urban Planning, 106(3), 262–270. https://doi.org/10.1016/j.landurbplan.2012.03.010

9. Han KT, Ruan LW, Liao LS. Effects of Indoor Plants on Human Functions: A Systematic Review with Meta-Analyses. Int J Environ Res Public Health. 2022 Jun 17;19(12):7454. doi: 10.3390/ijerph19127454. PMID: 35742700; PMCID: PMC9224521.

10. Kuo, F.E., and W.C. Sullivan. 2001. Environment and Crime in the Inner City: Does Vegetation Reduce Crime? Environment and Behavior 33, 3:343-367.

11. Brooks, H.L., Rushton, K., Lovell, K. et al. The power of support from companion animals for people living with mental health problems: a systematic review and narrative synthesis of the evidence. BMC Psychiatry 18, 31 (2018). https://doi.org/10.1186/s12888-018-1613-2

merely biological, clinical, or psychological facts, not theological ones. The theologians of the Pagan, indigenous and Eastern religions would argue otherwise.

Among ancient animistic and polytheistic religions, weaving has been used as an analogy for the interconnected fates, and the interdependent existence, of all beings. This metaphor has been remarkably widespread, from the imagery of Indra's net of jewels, which is used in some strains of Buddhism to describe the interdependence of the existence of all beings, to the use of woven patterns by multiple American Indian tribes to represent the web of life, to the images of "threads of fate" which are interwoven to create the tapestry of existence which is found in multiple European cultures.

The interdependence and interconnectedness of all beings is considered a theological truth in these religions. These peoples who lived close to their sources of food were aware of not only the spiritual and psychological effects of other species and individuals on a person's being, but also of the physical interdependence of different species. The power these species held to bestow death or survival on our ancestors, and our own ability to take action to sustain their lives, made the necessity of a reciprocal partnership between us obvious.

We now know that such reciprocal partnerships form the basis of all ecology, with major changes and disasters occurring when one species in an environment disappears or changes its behavior so that it is no longer fulfilling the needs of another. While change is not always bad—in fact, it is the engine that drives the creation of new things—major changes to our ecosystems result in mass death events within them more often than we'd like.

This is what many environmental scientists now fear may happen to humanity in the coming century if we do not change our way. So many species within our food web are disappearing, or markedly changing their behavior due to climate change, that scientists are increasingly unsure that we will be able to compensate for these changes using technology.

We are increasingly unsure that we will continue to be able to feed our children if we do not begin to reverse our behavior which is destructive to our climate systems and our partner species.[12][13] Beyond the obvious threats of climate change, many scientists and activists are concerned about the effect of human activities on "keystone species"—species whose well-being turns out to be vital to the well-being of an entire ecosystem, and all the species in it. Historically, keystone species have often been identified only after it was too late and their decline or extinction began to cause mass death events in other plant or animal species.[14] This raises the specter that the collapse of human food webs could occur in a sudden and unpredictable manner as damage to other species from human activity progresses.

Treating other species as beings with rights, then, increasingly appears to be more than a matter of moral or ethical nicety. Prioritizing the rights of our divine kin would likely produce the same actions that are necessary for our own self-preservation. This is the nature of the web of life: when one node in the web is damaged, all other nodes are

---

12. United Nations. The world's food supply is made insecure by climate change. United Nations. https://www.un.org/en/academic-impact/worlds-food-supply-made-insecure-climate-change

13. Climate change, Global Food Security, and the U.S. Food System. USDA. (n.d.). https://www.usda.gov/oce/energy-and-environment/food-security

14. What is a keystone species, and why do they matter?. World Economic Forum. https://www.weforum.org/agenda/2021/09/what-is-a-keystone-species/

affected. And we are one such node. It makes sense, then, not just from an idealistic perspective, but from a survival perspective, to return to our ancestors' ways of honoring our fellow species.

If some theologies wish to call this heresy, idolatry, or demonism, they may do so at their own risk. I personally find it difficult to justify the demonization of loving, nurturing relationships with our fellow beings.

Putting this theology into practice in the modern world is exceedingly complicated. This is more true than ever in an industrialized and globalized world where thousands of workers, plants, and animals who we do not see or know anything about may be involved in an operation as basic as producing the food we eat. Many critics of animistic and ecocentric theologies have claimed that following these ideas to their natural conclusion would result in reduced conversion of natural resources into wealth and reduced levels of material prosperity for humans.

In a way, this may be true. Living with respect for all life is likely to make some luxuries less affordable and narrow the selection of goods available to us on the global marketplace somewhat. It may also lead to decreases in GDP. But let us consider *why* that is. If drops are seen in economic activity, it will be because we are leaving the riches of our world in their most spiritually fulfilling forms: the forms of our fellow living beings, and our spiritual relationships with them, instead of cannibalizing these to produce financial wealth.

That is a trade-off I think we would all be happier taking. We will discuss a few practical steps we can take in this direction in Chapter 8.

Of course, the web of life does not refer *only* to our relationships with other species. These are simply the relationships which will kill the largest numbers of our people fastest if we continue to neglect them. The theological truth of interdependence also shapes our personal lives, and can give us the power to shape ourselves and our communities when used wisely.

A Message from a Goddess

While I was writing this book, I had an interesting experience. I was invited to compose a message from the Goddess to the Parliament of World Religions taking place in my home city in a few months. I determined that the best way to do this would be to revisit the place where the Goddess first visited me, and where She spoke most clearly to me during my younger years. But as I approached the place of our first meeting, something entirely unexpected happened.

A storm blew up, seemingly out of nowhere. A big one. When I began my journey, the day was bright and sunny. When I arrived at the closest road to the nature area that was my destination, a dark cumulonimbus had blown up in the west. And not just that.

As I walked toward the spot appointed for our meeting despite the promise of a storm—the Goddess had communicated with me through storms before—a perfectly round cloud dropped down over the nature area. It was a wall cloud, the precursor to a tornado. As wind whipped past me, rising up into the cloud—an updraft, the stuff of which funnel clouds are made—my phone began to blare an alarm in my pocket. A tornado warning for the area had been declared at the exact time and place appointed for our meeting.

As I stood underneath the wall cloud, looking up at it and watching the wind whip at the trees, I felt very helpless. I had grown up on the corner of tornado alley and seen, on one occasion, an entire solid brick high school demolished by an F5 tornado. Even if I could get back to a shelter in time, I knew that would not completely exempt me from annihilation.

And there was another interesting layer to this event. When I was growing up, property-damaging tornadoes did not happen in my home state. I had been taught in elementary school that tornadoes were indeed possible in North America only during a certain span of months. When my home state experienced our first tornado warning in my memory in 2012, I laughed at the foolishness of the precaution. Then a colleague of mine got home from work to find that part of her house was gone. The existence of tornadoes posing threats to human life in my home state was new, very real, and likely a consequence of human-caused climate change.

And so the message from the Goddess was clear: for all humanity's mastery of certain technologies, we are still very much at the mercy of nature. The wind and waves will always be more powerful than we are, as will the sheer vast expanse and titanic forces involved in our creation on this Earth.

Those who study other planets are even more aware of how tremendously merciful our planet is than most: our ribbon of atmosphere is incredibly thin; the balance of chemicals, pressure, and radiation which permit our existence are in an extremely fine balance; a tiny, temperate sliver of the band of environmental conditions seen on other worlds.

It is easy to see how we can become confused, feeling ourselves to be impervious, because we have overcome several natural limitations using technology in recent millennia. But our power has grown faster than our wisdom, and we now face a point where our power to damage the systems we rely on for survival outstrips our power to protect ourselves.

If we wish to survive much longer, then, we must turn our power to repairing the damage we have done to the systems which allow us to exist, which are so much larger than ourselves. Just because tornadoes are rare does not mean we can allow ourselves to feel invulnerable to the consequences of our actions under the open sky. It only takes one storm to end a life, and there is no getting such a life back.

Indigenous religions have always been acutely aware of this, perhaps because their oral traditions reach back longer than our written records. They have seen the climate change; many of today's indigenous traditions appear to have some sort of oral tradition which reaches back at least to the end of the last Ice Age. Indeed, the universality of flood stories is now believed by some anthropologists to be related to some catastrophic rises in sea level which may have occurred when ice dams broke or tsunamis were triggered by melt-related landslides 5,000-10,000 years ago.[15]

10,000 years ago, our power as a species was already growing. Scientists now believe that Ice Age humans were likely responsible for the extinction of the megafauna such as mammoths, mastodons, aurochs, and big cats who used to cover the globe.[16] Perhaps this is why the peoples who live closest to the Earth had already developed teachings that we were responsible for maintaining the welfare of our fellow beings if we wished to preserve our own food sources thousands of years ago.

---

15. Newitz, A. (2012, September 3). Ancient flood myths may have a basis in geological history. Gizmodo. https://gizmodo.com/ancient-flood-myths-may-have-a-basis-in-geological-hist-5940112

16. Ritchie, H. (2022, November 30). Did humans cause the quaternary megafauna extinction?. Our World in Data. https://ourworldindata.org/quaternary-megafauna-extinction#:~:text=There%20have%20now%20been%20many,by%20climate%20on%20its%20own.

Many indigenous peoples explicitly report a specific pact: their food species will allow certain members of their population to be harvested to feed humanity, if humanity will safeguard the continued existence of their own species. This agreement is often manifested in policies about where, when, and how it is permissible to harvest plants and animals and which sorts of animals and plants are allowed to be harvested in terms of their age, sex, and other characteristics, as well as in theological explanations for these agreements and religious rituals which serve to keep the survival and theological importance of these relationships in the forefront of the hearts and minds of the people.

For this reason, many policy experts have recommended that indigenous autonomy and land sovereignty be protected as a means of protecting our own global food supply.[17] And it seems neither safe nor fair to entrust *only* indigenous peoples with these duties of stewardship. Instead, it seems necessary that we adopt similar practices and attitudes of responsibility ourselves to safeguard our children's futures.

For indigenous peoples, and increasingly for the Pagans of today, these relationships and rituals are not merely practical in nature. Many Pagan and indigenous theologies teach, quite literally, that animals are other types of people. Many indigenous and religious leaders refer to other species as "peoples," and many Pagan teachers speak of lack of contact with our divine kin, our siblings in the family of living beings created by the gods, being related to modern human feelings of loneliness and alienation.

---

17. United Nations. Challenges and opportunities for Indigenous Peoples' sustainability | DISD. United Nations. https://www.un.org/development/desa/dspd/2021/04/indigenous-peoples-sustainability/

Anyone who has personally experienced communion with a plant, forest, animal, or weather system can speak to the profound power and fulfillment contained in these experiences of communion. There is mounting scientific evidence for the fact that the mere presence of plants, animals, and fresh air change a human's neurological state, making mental illness and crime less likely while altruistic behavior and experiences of joy become more likely.

Scientists are still elucidating possible biochemical messenger pathways by which this could occur. But from a theologian's perspective, the claim that humans need our divine siblings to be happy and healthy appears to be validated. The matter of honoring, nurturing, and protecting our divine kin, then, is not *merely* one of survival. It is a matter of our individual well-being; of our ability to experience the fullness of joy and love that human life was intended to contain.

Attributing theological importance to the existence of other species, and to our relationships with them, would appear useful on many counts then. Unfortunately, these ideas have often been actively demonized as blasphemy and idolatry by the colonial religions which have now spread to cover much of the planet.

Indigenous ideas about our divine relationships with other species, and the rituals designed to honor and renew them, have often been actively banned as demonism and heresy by religious leaders. It has been primarily Christianity and Islam which have historically banned and punished these "Pagan" activities as alleged signs of an untrustworthy and immoral theology, but, any colonial religion or philosophy is vulnerable to demonizing such life-sustaining ideas and rituals. Many speculate that this is because such relationships are inconvenient to those driven by a desire for power and profit.

It is not convenient for an invading army to be concerned about maintaining right relationship with the local plants, animals and nature spirits; in fact, it is ideal for the army to be told that they are morally justified in conquering the inhabitants because the inhabitants are idolatrous devil-worshippers who commit the grave sin of attributing theological importance to their ecosystems.

Similarly, it is not convenient for a billionaire whose wealth derives from the harvesting and sale of natural resources to be concerned with such relationships. When unlimited harvest means unlimited wealth, a theology may arise by which it is wicked and evil to wish to limit the harvest, and it is blasphemous to suggest that humans are powerful enough to alter what is ultimately God's decision about whether to provide for future generations or not.

I would argue that these motivations are the reason why beliefs about humanity being in a spiritual and theologically important relationship with other species has dropped off in recent millennia. With the advent of technology which could produce short-term growth in the wealth and power of individuals, the incentive of wealthy and powerful individuals to demonize those who would limit their wealth and power grew.

Ask yourself: are such people still exerting influence on my religious community today? Do your leaders still bow to politicians or wealthy individuals who tell us it is wrong to limit the economic activities of corporations, or the military activities of war? Is your theology shaped, ultimately, by the teachings of your God, or by the teachings of humans who claim to speak authoritatively about God's will even as they demonize and authorize the destruction of the world and the peoples He made?

Chapter Five

Pagan Ethics and Values

One frequent question is how Pagans arrive at their values and ethics in the absence of a holy text that is considered infallible. For those who do have such a book, the question of how a person decides what is right and wrong without one can be confusing. Common strains of argument against atheism and polytheism include the argument that a person can't know what is right and wrong without the help of a single divine authority.

To that, I say this: how did people know to follow Jesus? Was it because he was aligned with the prevailing religious teachings of his time? He wasn't. Why, then, did his teachings and actions seem obviously morally good to the many people who chose to follow him?

For scientists who study human behavior and for contemplatives who study the human heart, it is not difficult to see that there is a nearly universal morality of care which has formed the primary basis for the laws of religions around the world; and against which the moral success of a religion may be judged. This principle, which I refer to as the law of love, is demonstrably *the* driving force behind modern advances in ethics and morality including those prominent in modern Pagan and atheist circles.

With hundreds of thousands of Pagan religions in the historical record, it is impossible to encompass the ethics and values of every single one of them. But it is possible to make a few general statements about values shared by most modern Pagan faiths, and values shared particularly by the people who are practicing Paganism today.

Love is the Law

There is encouraging news from the world of sociological research. In general, human societies seem to be moving more toward values that prioritize the freedom and well-being of humans, or of all living things.

Most modern Pagans espouse high levels of what are described by the World Values Survey as "secular-rational" and "self-expression" values. These are values which, in short, espouse the use of rationality rather than tradition to find ways of life that maximize the well-being of living things, and which seek to maximize the rights of individual beings to live as they wish to the greatest extent possible.

Let's talk a little bit about the World Values Survey because it's wonderful.

The World Values Survey is a large-scale scientific undertaking to survey hundreds of thousands of people from across dozens of different countries and attempt to develop a systematic way of classifying values across cultures. The Survey's work is truly fascinating and can be utilized for purposes up to and including predicting election results. It is to my knowledge the largest attempt to systematically collect and compare data about how people think and feel about ethics and morality across global cultures, and in that respect, its work is invaluable.

For our purposes, what is most interesting is the two axes along which Survey scientists have classified human values. These are:

- Survival vs. self-expression values. On the "survival" end of this spectrum lie cultures who value basic physical safety above all else. These are often cultures which exist in harsh or dangerous conditions, and which subsequently advocate for behavior that reduces risk and optimizes chances of survival over behavior that expresses a person's unique inner self. At the opposite end of the spectrum lie those who believe people should be allowed to live as they wish to the greatest extent physically possible. These views often arise in societies that have enjoyed long periods of material prosperity and safety, and lead to discussions about how to best create protocols, cultures, and legal systems that maximize the freedom and autonomy of individuals to the greatest possible extent.

- Traditional vs. secular-rational values. On the "traditional" end of this spectrum lie cultures and individuals which believe things must always be done in accordance with tradition, and that bad things will result if traditions are broken. This view also is more common in societies with conditions of material danger or scarcity, perhaps because traditions passed down from previous generations can convey a significant survival advantage under such circumstances. On the secular-rational end of the spectrum are people who believe that the best way forward should be arrived at by using the most up-to-date available knowledge to design systems which maximize the well-being of all humans, or all living beings of all species, depending on the strain of secular-rational thought. As in the case of self-expression values, this view is most commonly held by people who have enjoyed long periods of prosperity and safety and who have been able to turn their minds away from basic survival and toward optimization.[1]

Modern Pagans are particularly likely to hold self-expression and secular-rational values, because many of them left the religions or belief systems of their births over objections that these did not adequately provide for the freedom or well-being of living beings. Many modern Pagans cite frustration with religious laws which seemed to limit self-expression, or which science and logic suggested were doing more harm than good to their communities.

I believe it is important that leaders of established religions consider these realities seriously. Too often I have heard religious leaders express the belief that young people were leaving their religions because they had become *too* progressive and not traditional enough. Yet, at least in the United States, the majority of Americans under the age of 40 who no longer identify as Christian have been very clear about their reasons for leaving.

I don't believe it would be unreasonable to postulate that between 80% to 90% of Americans under 40 would report sexism, homophobia, transphobia, and other religious teachings which caused harm as their major reasons for leaving the religions of their birth. While religious leaders sometimes paint young people who have left their congregations as selfish libertines, my experience interviewing hun-

---

1. World values survey association. WVS Database. https://www.worldvaluessurvey.org/WVSContents.jsp

dreds of such individuals has been that the vast majority left because of perceived harms their religious leaders were doing to their loved ones and community members, *not* because of personal frustration at being asked to follow religious rules.

It is my opinion that religious leaders should seriously consider this data in their assessment of human nature, and of the impact their own religious organizations are having on their communities.

These findings from my own interview processes are supported by the much larger volume of data and the much more scientific approach of the World Values Survey, as discussed above. The societies with the highest levels of secular-rational and self-expression values are also those with the lowest levels of participation in large religious organizations.

But this does not mean that people who hold these values cannot be religious. Indeed, I would hazard an assertion that modern Pagan communities have been largely shaped by secular-rational and self-expression values, forming in many cases as alternatives to religious communities which reject certain types of social progress and ignore certain humanitarian and environmental crises.

I should note that some modern Pagans may object to this characterization, since some Pagan traditions do highly value tradition and the guidance of elders and adherence to time-honored traditions, especially those with recent indigenous roots. In fact, it is accurate to say that many modern Pagan communities are using traditions and teachings which are older (and therefore more traditional?) than those espoused by the modern theologians of the largest world religions.

This is a valid objection and warrants further study, since almost all of the data from the World Values Survey stems from the study of non-indigenous religious traditions, which rely heavily on written dogmas and often view all attempts at innovation or social progress as violations of their traditions.

Indeed, the term "secular-rational" may originate from the arguments of some prominent religious leaders that rational approaches to problem solving can only be practiced within secular societies who are not bound by religious traditions. Criticism of secular societies which "violate religious law" by advancing human rights or environmental protections unfortunately remain common among the leadership of some of the world's largest religious organizations.

However, I would suggest to the authors of the World Values Survey that these leaders do not represent *all* religious traditions and that the term "rational" would suffice to describe these values which are perfectly capable of being espoused by traditional religious communities.

In any case, since many modern Pagans are people who have left other religions due to perceived failures to support personal autonomy and freedom or prioritize the use of rationality to solve humanitarian problems, levels of secular-rational and self-expression values in Pagan communities are high. This has led to a religious community culture which is quick to adopt new frameworks for maximizing individual rights and the welfare of living beings.

Some modern Pagan communities are creating truly novel, and arguably morally better ways of being, by combining cutting-edge modern protocols for the respect of individual rights and autonomy with ancient wisdom which respects the individual rights and autonomy of non-human beings.

Pagan communities which practice both consent culture and animism, for example, offer an inspirational window into what is possible for human societies when our principles prioritize respect for the freedom and dignity of all life and extend that respect to our fellow species and natural processes. I see these communities as being the most advanced and promising examples of how future human societies can cultivate respect for individuals and respect for other living beings while living in spiritually whole and materially sustainable communities together.

Promising work is also being done in incorporating restorative justice models which empower victims of mistreatment while allowing offenders to reform and re-integrate into communities and the cultures of some Pagan communities.

While it would take entire volumes of ethnography to document the innovations I've seen in modern Pagan communities which are informed both by activist groups working to solve modern human rights problems and indigenous peoples who are willing to share their ancient wisdom; suffice to say that modern Pagan communities are well worth studying to learn how a better world is possible. These religious communities which in many cases are creating their group protocols almost from scratch in the absence of established religious authorities have a unique opportunity to fully realize modern understandings about morality and ethics.

These Pagan converts often very explicitly espouse self-expression and secular-rational values. One common idea in many strains of Paganism, both ancient and modern, is the idea that each person born is a unique manifestation of the Divine, who is constructed specifically to experience, create, and accomplish certain things.

Modern Pagan communities are often highly oriented toward supporting individual members in empowering and manifesting their true selves, with their only major taboos being on behavior that harms other living beings. To this end, these communities are often strongly oriented to "consent culture"—the idea that individuals should be able to decide and consent to what happens to them to the highest possible extent, to the point that consent becomes almost the only meaningful social norm within the community.

In communities oriented around consent culture, the appropriateness of gender roles, sexual behavior, and relationships are based almost entirely on whether all parties involved consent to these arrangements willingly rather than based on externally imposed laws or norms. Modern standards related to boundaries and consent are often even enforced with deities; with members often being counseled not to work with deities who don't respect their boundaries and consent and to instead seek out deities they feel comfortable with.

All of this is dictated by the law of love, in combination with the idea that individual humans are unique manifestations of the Divine. The combination of these two ideas produces communities in which *the* major priority is supporting the growth and welfare of members, and even of outsiders to the extent that the community has excess resources. Many modern Pagan groups are involved in fundraising for various humanitarian and environmental causes in addition to providing spiritual services to local community members in need.

While this does not describe *all* Pagan communities—a task that would be impossible due to the infinite diversity among Pagans—this does describe several large Pagan communities I have worked with, and those founded by pioneering Pagan theologians such as Starhawk.

It is possible that as the decades pass, Pagan communities may shift more toward traditional values as they become increasingly interested in exploring the traditions of their pre-Christian ancestors. Some communities which self-identify as Pagan already abide by more restrictive traditional norms about sex, gender, and relationships for example than those described above, and Pagan communities have appeared to show more interest, rather than less, in researching the traditions of their pre-colonial ancestors as the 21st century has progressed.

However, it is interesting to note that some of these traditions are, in fact, more pro-self-expression and more trusting of individual discernment than the Western traditions of the last few centuries. The archaeological record shows that many pre-Christian and pre-Muslim societies, for example, embraced much wider ranges of behavior from people of all genders, much wider ranges of sexual behavior and relationships, and more genders than the more recent Christian and Muslim societies. And even most Pagans of today profess that they do not seek to recreate an ancient tradition perfectly—this would not be possible, since the conditions under which their ancient ancestors lived no longer exist.

Instead, many Pagan organizers of today profess a desire to create a culture that is heavily informed by ancient practices, by timeless Pagan ideas such as the divinity of the the natural world, the ensouled species of the natural world as humanity's divine family, the nurturing relationship between deities and Their children, *and* by modern scientific knowledge and ethical developments.

In the words of the Celtic Reconstructionism Gateway, "By studying the old manuscript sources and the regional folklore, combining this information with mystical and ecstatic practice, and working together to weed out the non-Celtic elements that can arise, we are nurturing what still lives and helping the polytheistic Celtic traditions grow strong and whole again.

"We approach this in part by trying to envision what different Celtic Paganisms might look like today if they had been uninterrupted by Christianity, much as Hinduism has changed over the centuries, remaining the same religion but changing in form with the changing times."[2]

While the complexity of the moral calculations involved in running a community based on consent culture and the seeming unpredictability of relying heavily on individual discernment sound chaotic to those who espouse traditional and survival values, these approaches seem to have a high appeal to those who desire to live *only* under the Law of Love without other, potentially conflicting rules and edicts.

These secular-rational approaches also seem to aid in the prioritization of problems which the modern world is just rediscovering, such as the problems of environmental destruction and climate change, by allowing for the possibility that morally important issues may have been missed or misunderstood by past generations, and that some of the most important moral issues of our time may not be the same issues that our parents and grandparents were concerned with.

Pagan Values Around Religious Experience

Modern Pagans do tend to put a great deal of stock in individual discernment. In fact, there is some suggestion that this is historical: many Pagan authors and religious leaders refused to write their teachings down, even when systems of writing were available in their lands at the time.

A few went on record as saying that this was due to a belief that religious knowledge must be conveyed through firsthand experience, and

---

2. Price, K.. The CR FAQ - An introduction to Celtic Reconstructionist Paganism - so what is Celtic Reconstructionism?. A Celtic Reconstructionist Gateway. https://www.paganachd.com/faq/whatiscr.html

that if written versions of religious teachings became available people may begin to rely on these writings more than on direct experience of life or of the Divine. In their minds, this would be disastrous: there was no truly accurate map to the Divine outside of reality itself, so reliance on an imperfect holy text was likely to produce significant misinterpretations of how to conduct spiritual relationships properly.

One Daoist philosopher was famously coerced into writing down approximations of his beliefs, and opened this approximation with "The way that can be told is not the eternal Way; the name that can be named is not the eternal Name."[3]

Regardless of the historicity of this claim that ancient Pagan teachers refrained from writing down their teachings because they valued individual discernment highly, modern Pagans demonstrably do value individual discernment above adherence to written texts.

Indeed, it is interesting to consider that a huge proportion of modern Pagans became Pagan after having religious experiences which did not match what was prescribed in the written texts of their religions. This phenomenon has been so widespread for so long that criticism of people who rely on personal religious experiences instead of religious texts for their theological worldview can be found in the writings of some of the most prominent Christian authors of the 20th century.[4]

I can offer a personal window into what this looks like. As a child, I had profound religious experiences centering around religious ecstasies at religious beauty and a sense of communion with natural

---

3. Laozi, & Mitchell, S. (1988). Tao Te Ching. Harper & Row, Publishers.

4. Hambrick, B.. C.S. Lewis on theology as experience and map. Brad Hambrick. https://bradhambrick.com/lewisontheology/

phenomena. I was also on occasion able to see spiritual energies that I eventually realized matched the descriptions of auras and Qi given by religious traditions other than my own. This culminated in visions of a Goddess who gave me the strongest religious calling I have ever experienced in my life to date.

These visions were so clearly of the same nature as the religious visions chronicled by the saints who achieved communion with God according to the church I was raised in that I knew them to be religious experiences. But these experiences were treated with fear, suspicion, and discouragement by adult members of my church when I spoke of them. These adults did not know how to reconcile these experiences with their own theology, which did not admit the existence of auras or Qi and had a deep sense of unease about the possibilities of idolatry, blasphemy, and demonic deceptions.

The adults of my church ultimately concluded that my religious experiences must have been demonic in nature, since they did not fit into the church's theology and were threatening to many of the religious and political stances which the church leadership believed were necessary to ensure the supremacy of Christianity in my society. I was subsequently told that my religious visions were either demonic attacks or mere effects of an overactive imagination, and that I ought not pursue my divine calling which the church deemed clearly illegitimate as it was not in line with their own theology.

It is easy to see how such behavior could actively destroy individuals' sensitivity to divine callings, and ultimately, their relationships with the spirit world. So much of how we interpret subjective experience is based on feedback from other people, especially if we grow up in traditions and societies which teach us that our own judgment is susceptible to sinful corruption and cannot be trusted.

To me, it is one of the great tragedies of imperial religions that they appear to actively destroy the very personal relationship with the Divine which they claim to exist in order to facilitate. The obsession with control and the policing of human behavior and religious experience actively destroys human relationships with their fellow spiritual beings and with the divine source of all life.

Pagan communities have put into use specific protocols around discussing personal religious experiences in ways that both maximize self-expression and avoid dogmatic power struggles that can occur when some people have religious experiences that they feel give them license to tell others what to do.

In Pagan communities, the abbreviation "UPG" is often used for "unverified personal gnosis." The "unverified" in UPG refers to the belief that personal religious experiences are just that: personal. "Personal gnosis," of course, refers to the Pagan belief that the divine regularly speaks to individuals to help them expand their knowledge, understanding, and relationship with the divine as a matter of course. Religious visions are considered the norm rather than the exception in many Pagan religious communities.

Modern Pagans cultivate an awareness that all divine messages humans receive are filtered through our biological brains, and so our interpretation of them may be influenced by our own cultural and personal preconceptions. For this reason, instances of UPG are often brought to one's Pagan community for discussion and assistance in interpretation.

The term "unverified personal gnosis" allows Pagan communities to simultaneously acknowledge these religious experiences as legitimate divine revelations, and subject them to individual and community discernment in a way that minimizes conflict and does not give those who have religious visions power or moral authority over other community members. In this way, religious visions can be acknowledged and embraced as important without creating problematic dogmas or power dynamics.

I sometimes think that other religious communities could benefit greatly from this framework, as so many conflicts between religious leaders could potentially be talked out in a community setting which acknowledges both the likelihood of a legitimate divine revelation and any possible personal or cultural biases that may be influencing its interpretation in this way. Religious leaders facing struggles around seemingly conflicting or heretical divine revelations within their communities may wish to research this approach. Pagan leaders are often happy to help train leaders of other religions in these protocols and discussion techniques.

Pagan communities often cultivate methods such as trance work, hypnosis, and guided meditation which seem fairly reliable at producing religious experiences in times of need or when personal growth is sought. But more interesting is the fact that most Pagan converts come to Paganism because they have *already* had naturally occuring religious experiences which appeared incompatible with the religion or worldview they were raised with, but which seemed compatible with the religious imagery and values espoused by Pagan communities.

It is easy to see how the Pagan values described here make it easy for Pagans to embrace people with wide varieties of religious experiences in addition to people of all sexes, genders, sexual orientations, and relationship styles. When the expression of the divine spark within the individual is given theological importance, and relationships are judged based primarily on the harm or good they do to the people in them, it is easy to create communities in which all those who treat others with respect are welcome.

Pagan communities have distinguished themselves in recent decades as safe havens for LGBTQ+ people and people whose sexualities or relationship styles may need to be concealed to avoid rejection in many other religious communities.

It was interesting to me to observe that when I moved from a Christian to a Buddhist religious community, I found myself in the midst of a religious community which had openly gay and lesbian members for the first time in my life. These relationships would have been categorically rejected by the religion of my birth, especially among clergy, and in this Zen Buddhist community the polar opposite was true. Several students in the local monastery's seminary program were in fact married to same-sex spouses.

The increased diversity I observed continued as I moved from Buddhist into Pagan circles. In the Pagan religious community which I ultimately called home, a large proportion of congregation members were trans or of nonbinary genders, and I soon learned that there were many trans and polyamorous families who were lovingly embraced by the religious community.

I have come to deeply appreciate the freedom afforded by Pagan religious communities which use consent culture values instead of prevailing social norms to determine right and wrong, and which embrace all relationships of love and nurturance.

The opportunities for spiritual growth and support network growth which are afforded by this approach are drastically underappreciated, and there is a school of historical scholarship which suggests that such gender identities and relationship arrangements have been discouraged by religious and political authorities specifically as a means of maintaining control over the spiritual and material lives of individuals. We will discuss this more in Chapter 7.

So how do Pagans think about sex and gender, and what can other religions add to their own protocols and understandings from Pagan gender theology?

Chapter Six

Pagan Gender Theology

Gender and the divisions that come with it have been a major source of humanitarian controversy in recent centuries. As human societies become more preoccupied with conquest and the hoarding of material wealth, they tend to develop stricter and stricter ideas about what genders are valid and what people of different genders should be allowed to do. In many cases these ideas have been elevated to the status of theology, with claims that God created only two genders, and did so for the express purpose that they produce as many offspring together as possible.

These societies may punish people who are deemed to have violated these divinely ordained gender roles by partaking in "inappropriate" activities, and this punitive attitude toward individuals based on gender roles has been a source of major human rights violations over the years. It has led to the violent punishment of many victimless "sins," the removal of legal rights from different gender groups, and fear mongering that human rights campaigns will ultimately damage society by allowing people to partake in activities that are not appropriate for their gender.

It is my desire to see this end, and I believe that the gender theologies espoused by many Pagans today provide a way to do that.

Even Pagan gender theology is the subject of much controversy because early modern Pagan gender theology was heavily influenced by Christianity. The theologians of the early Goddess movement made compelling arguments for the moral and theological importance of revering God's feminine side and feminine attributes as co-equal with His masculine side.

The theology and community practices developed by Goddess movement Pagan circles was deeply healing and inspiring for women and theologians of other religions alike at a time when women were still commonly openly demonized if they attempted to take part in life beyond their assigned roles as caregivers for men and children.

At a time when women were often described as sinful and weak in church sermons, and were not allowed to have a bank account without a male co-signer in many U.S. states, the image of God as a loving Earth Mother was transformative in many ways. But this was not by any means the end of modern developments in Pagan gender theology. Pagans of the Millennial and Zoomer generations have been quick to point out that Goddess movement conceptions of gender theology still match the 20th century Christian in many ways.

Goddess theology has expanded ideas about the spiritual nature and acceptable social roles of men and women significantly, but have continued to lean heavily on images of women as the more caregiving and nurturing sex, giving central theological importance to women's roles as birthers of children, and have continued to characterize men as the more violent and forceful sex. Some strains of Goddess theology have even suggested that men are the less trustworthy sex, citing damage done under patriarchy and claiming that women are inherently more peaceful and nurturing decision-makers.

This has led to conflicts with younger generations of Pagans, who are concerned by what they perceive as attempts to continue enforcing patriarchal gender roles. The complete lack of mechanism for addressing people of trans and additional genders has also caused many intergenerational conflicts within the modern Pagan community, with some Goddess movement religious leaders insisting that people with penises not be allowed in women's spaces, while young Pagans overwhelmingly refuse to support religious spaces that exclude trans women.

There is a great deal to unpack about recent developments in gender theology, especially as some religious communities still struggle to conceive of God as anything other than a biological male and take literally scriptures suggesting that women should be unconditionally obedient to men, while others have long since moved to a place of revering God's masculine and feminine sides equally and are concerned with the continued stereotyping of men and women and the exclusion of other genders from 20th century Goddess theology.

Come with me as I tell you some stories of how Pagan communities have dealt with these challenges around gender, and the theologies underlying their approaches.

The 20th Century Goddess Movement

Arguably *the* major point of departure between Pagan and mainstream monotheistic theologies in the 20th century was the role of women in religious leadership. It is easy for many modern people to forget that, as recently as 50 or 60 years ago, women had almost no property rights and were themselves considered almost as property even in the legal systems of many parts of the United States and Western Europe.

Many of the founders of Paganism as we know it today grew up at a time when many families in the U.S. and Europe still felt that female children did not need higher education, as their primary purpose in life would be to get married and have children. Many of our mothers and grandmothers were denied college educations because their families refused to pay to educate a woman, and many entered the workforce at a time when women were not allowed to have their own bank accounts, or sometimes even jobs, due to cultural beliefs about women being weak, unreliable, or it being "improper" for women to engage in work other than the care of men and children.

These cultural beliefs, which often led to violent abuse of women and children, in which women were not empowered to end due to their financial dependence on men, were fueled in large part by patriarchal theologies. At this time in the United States and Western Europe, it was not uncommon for Christian religious leaders to openly speak about women being the morally, spiritually, and mentally weaker sex and being the gateway through which demonic influences could enter the world.

As recently as a few decades ago, the Biblical story of Adam and Eve was often cited as evidence that women could not be trusted to make decisions without the supervision of men, and that women's biological functions were a literal punishment from God for Eve's sin which resulted in the fall of humanity and the entire natural world.

When the first Wiccan covens in Britain and the Goddess Movement in the U.S. exploded onto the scene, they sent shockwaves through Western culture. Here were religious leaders who had devout followers, and who said that women were at least as capable of religious leadership as men. In fact, both movements explicitly envisioned God as a woman, arguing that it made more sense and was moral to envision God as a mother birthing life from Her own body and spirit than as a male craftsman.

Hundreds of thousands of women across the Western world bought books on Wicca, which instructed them in how to commune with the Goddess and how to use spiritual arts which had been forbidden by the monotheistic faiths to change their lives. In the United States, hundreds of thousands of women joined Goddess-centered religious congregations. The Goddess movement became so entwined with feminism, civil rights, and ecological activism that Pagan women's groups often facilitated rituals at protests and direct actions and started one of the first needle exchange programs to prevent the spread of HIV in the 1980s.[1,2]

With the support of the Goddess movement, archaeologists, authors, and theologians began to argue that there was compelling evidence for the historicity that the original religion of humanity was the worship of a benevolent Earth Mother Goddess, who birthed all living things as divine children.[3] Books were published about ancient cul-

---

1. Salomonsen, J. (2002). Enchanted feminism ritual, gender and divinity among the Reclaiming Witches of San Francisco. Routledge.

2. Starhawk. (1982). Dreaming the dark: Magic, sex, & politics. Beacon Press.

3. Sjöö, M., & Mor, B. (2012). The Great Cosmic Mother: Rediscovering The Religion of the Earth. HarperOne, an imprint of HarperCollinsPublishers.

tures which worshiped goddesses as supreme deities[4] and compelling fictional worlds were crafted showing what peaceful, Goddess-centered prehistoric religions might have looked like.[5]

While this view came surprisingly close to approximating the views of many indigenous cultures, the versions propagated in the 20th century also carried a heavy Christian influence.

Goddess theologians continued to teach that a woman's primary theological importance was her ability to bear children, though they elevated childbirth to the status of an act of divine creation of life and suggested that women were closer to God than men for this reason. In many cases, Goddess movement religious leaders continued to suggest that it was women's role in society to be nurturing and benevolent, while it was the work of men to be violent and forceful.

In many ways, the theology about gender was the same as in Christianity: the major difference was that those traits of biological women which were portrayed as marks of servitude and moral weakness in Christian patriarchy were now portrayed as marks of enlightenment and divinity.

The status of women had improved significantly, and it is arguable that a cultural shift away from punitive violence and toward venerating the creation and nurturing of life happened as a result of the Goddess movement as well. I do not believe it would be a stretch to credit the Goddess movement as a major influence on the decline in

---

4. Stone, M. (1978). When God was a Woman. Harcourt Brace Jovanovich.

5. Auel, J. M. (1983). The Valley of the Horses. Hodder and Stoughton. .

war and the improvement in the pace of ecological destruction in the Western world that took place in the second half of the 20th century.

This was all for the better. But developments in the theology and culture around gender were not done.

The New Wave of Feminism

The Millennial and Zoomer Pagans born in the West today were born into a world where the sort of sexism experienced by their mothers and grandmothers was often considered cartoonish and unrealistic. While some churches and even public schools continued to teach that certain activities were inappropriate for people with uteruses, those who fought such requirements in the courts and in the court of public opinion now usually won.

In the space of two generations, openly sexist teachings had come to be viewed as so morally repugnant that even patriarchal religious organizations took pains to avoid appearing to espouse them. In most of the Western world, it was now illegal to discriminate on the basis of sex in any legal matter, and programs specifically designed to encourage girls and women to enter traditionally male-dominated career fields were now common.

This was when other problems with our cultural ideas about gender began to come into sharp focus for the younger generations. A creeping sense that traditional gender roles were still causing serious problems began to dawn.

Young people compared notes and learned that many of their male friends and family had been punished as children for engaging in activities their parents found "too feminine," and young men reported still being told to "man up" and having violence and harassment against them minimized on the grounds that boys should be strong enough to "take it."

Some young women, on the other hand, reported being traumatized by older women trying to force them to embody their own ideas about more "enlightened" gender roles. It seemed that some 20th century feminists had grown up to pressure their daughters to either embrace or reject traditional femininity according to their mothers' gender ideology rather than according to the innate inclinations of the child. Some feminist mothers of the early 21st century appeared to view a rejection of traditional femininity as rooted in misogyny, while others said the same thing about women who embraced traditional femininity.

And as these younger generations reached puberty and adulthood, many began to become aware of a new issue. Some of our friends began reporting that they were deeply uncomfortable with the sex of the body they'd been born into, or that they were deeply uncomfortable being addressed as either male or female.

As it turned out, these two things were happening a *lot*. As young people compared notes, it began to seem possible that a significant percentage of people were deeply uncomfortable with the gender they'd been assigned at birth. And this discomfort was so bad that, in many of our friends, it had led to suicidal ideation and depression sufficient to destroy a person's academic career.

I was one of those Millennials who had no idea what to do when my first dear friend came out to me as transgender. I had become close with her because she was possibly the only other student at my high school who had undertaken serious study of both theology and science of her own accord and not as part of some assigned academic program.

I had known that something was *off* with her for some time, as she was one of the two highest-scoring students in my school on standardized tests for college entrance exams, but she was failing out of our shared classes. She seemed unable to motivate herself to do her schoolwork, and frequently refused to see or speak to me for days at a time because her view of her own future had become so bleak that she did not trust herself to treat me with respect.

When she told me that she thought she was a woman who had been born in the wrong body and she could not see herself continuing life as a man (she'd been presenting as male up to this point), I had no idea what to make of it. I had never even heard of gender dysphoria, either in my church or in my public school system. She had not told anyone the true source of her depression because she hadn't heard of it either. She knew enough to know that churches disapproved of gay people, and she couldn't imagine what they'd think of someone like her.

It soon became clear that I had no option but to support her in any way she asked: almost no one else was doing so, and her depression was the worst I'd ever seen. If someone didn't validate her feelings and support her in getting what she needed, she was going to die.

Upon consulting the teachings of my church, I found that they explicitly taught that there was no such thing as a trans gender identity. According to my church's teachings, gender transitions were "gravely disordered" and were violations of God's will. And of course, "violation of God's will" was synonymous with sin. It became clear that if my friend transitioned, she would be considered a grave sinner in the eyes of my church.

This helped precipitate my breakup with the church that had raised me. Telling me that I could never serve as clergy because women were not spiritually suited to perform sacraments had not been enough to do it. Telling me that my own religious visions were invalid and possibly demonic in origin and should be ignored had not been enough to do it. Telling me that what my friend needed to stay alive was a grave sin *was* enough to do it.

I want everyone to remember this when they are faced with arguments against gender confirmation care, for minors or adults. My friend managed to survive until the age of 18 without gender confirmation treatment, but she almost lost her college admission and her future career prospects because of the depression caused by her gender dysphoria. And she almost died.

Hundreds of thousands of similar testimonies abound, available to all in the information age if one only thinks to look for them. But these are generally ignored and sometimes actively concealed by political and religious leaders who are so convinced that their academic understanding of gender theology is correct that they are willing to sacrifice the lives of children who cannot live in the world they've created.

Fortunately, a religion exists which embraced trans gender identities, and which I was shocked to learn were also happy to embrace my own religious visions and the spiritual practices to which I had felt naturally drawn since I was a child. It turned out that I had, at some level, been Pagan all my life; I just hadn't realized it, because I had never been taught what Paganism was.

When I entered Pagan religious circles for the first time in the 2010s, I was thrilled to discover that they had, in many ways, answers for all my questions. They had drawn from world theologies and activism circles to find theologies and protocols best-suited to solve modern problems. On the matter of gender theology, a deep dive into religious history found that *most* pre-imperial cultures had recognized trans gender identities, and in many cases also additional genders.

In these cultures, what was happening to my friend would have been common knowledge. At puberty or older in many of these cultures, she would have been allowed to declare her gender identity and join a community of people like herself, who in many cultures would have been regarded as divinely called to religious or political leadership.[6][7][8] In historical cultures which fully lived the reality of God transcending all genders, people who didn't fit neatly into male or female slots were often regarded as being closer to God by virtue of being more able to understand this transcendent perspective.

While many of the mainstream gender theologies of the 20th century taught that the primary purpose of sex and gender was the physical, biological creation of new life, these theologies recognized that gender was more than biological reproductive capacity. With different genders came different ways of being, different mental, emotional, and embodied states.

---

6. David, A. (2018, December 30). Ancient civilization in Iran recognized transgender people 3,000 years ago, study suggests. Haaretz.com. https://www.haaretz.com/archaeology/2018-12-30/ty-article-magazine/.premium/ancient-civilization-in-iran-recognized-transgender-people-study-suggests/0000017f-e0fc-d7b2-a77f-e3ffb5fb0000

7. Two-Spirit: Health Resources. Lesbian, Gay, Bisexual and Transgender Health. (n.d.). https://www.ihs.gov/lgbt/health/twospirit/

8. McCarthy, J. (2014, April 18). A journey of pain and beauty: On becoming transgender in India. NPR. https://www.npr.org/sections/parallels/2014/04/18/304548675/a-journey-of-pain-and-beauty-on-becoming-transgender-in-india

Ancient traditions aligned with clinical data in suggesting that in most cases these were strongly correlated to reproductive anatomy, but that gender identity also dwelt somewhere else in the brain or spirit.[9] And while modern clinical perspectives viewed gender dysphoria as a biological mistake, the development of gender in the brain which was not compatible with the reproductive organs, these Pagan theologies viewed it as a divine gift.

In their view, gender identities which crossed or transcended the norm created the opportunity for greater understanding. A person who experienced both masculine and feminine mental, emotional, and embodied states, or neither, could add perspectives on God, humanity, and life on this Earth that purely male and female experiences alone could not yield.

It turned out that many ancient cultures had practiced gender confirmation and reassignment as a matter of course. The practice of social gender transitions and sometimes using herbs or surgery to induce hormonal masculinization or feminization was documented in early Canaanite and Jewish scriptures, and procedures for performing

---

9. Olson, K. R. (2017, September 1). When sex and gender collide. Scientific American. https://www.scientificamerican.com/article/when-sex-and-gender-collide/

divine gender transition rituals were found in millennia-old scriptures from Greece to Sumer to North and South America.[10][11][12]

Modern Pagan researchers had discovered that these experiences had always existed throughout human history, and had been systematically suppressed almost exclusively in societies which were obsessed with conquest and the accumulation of material wealth. We'll discuss the reasons for this in Chapter 7.

For now, know that by reviving traditions so old and forbidden they had been effectively forgotten by mainstream culture, modern Pagan communities had been able to solve a pressing humanitarian crisis and revive truly transcendent understandings of God and gender at the same time.

Let's take a moment to explore the theological implications of trans and nonbinary gender identities, and how they can help us all to transcend enforced gender roles and become more spiritually whole.

How Many Genders Are There, and Why?

---

10. Crocq MA. How gender dysphoria and incongruence became medical diagnoses - a historical review. Dialogues Clin Neurosci. 2022 Jun 1;23(1):44-51. doi: 10.1080/19585969.2022.2042166. PMID: 35860172; PMCID: PMC9286744.

11. Daniels, M. (2021, June 30). Ancient Mesopotamian transgender and non-binary identities. Academus Education. https://www.academuseducation.co.uk/post/ancient-mesopotamian-transgender-and-non-binary-identities

12. Two-Spirit: Health Resources. Lesbian, Gay, Bisexual and Transgender Health. (n.d.). https://www.ihs.gov/lgbt/health/twospirit/

A lynchpin of many patriarchal theologies is the idea that God created two sexes for the purposes of biological reproduction—and that all activities in life should be geared toward this goal. This is the view of traditional gender roles which punishes children for engaging in activities considered inappropriate for their sex practically from birth due to concern that children may become "confused" and unable to to perform their assigned duties later in life if allowed to indulge in cross-gender activities.

We now know that this may be an active attempt to suppress knowledge of trans gender identities, since clinical evidence suggests that engaging in childhood activities that are deemed cross-gender rarely results in serious long-term behavioral changes—unless the child is trans.

In recent decades, clinical researchers have found that children with trans gender identities often behave from an early age as the gender they identify with internally, not the gender they are assigned at birth.[13] The harsh punishment of cross-gender behavior in childhood, then, is likely a specific attempt to force trans children to conform to the roles expected of them by society based on their reproductive capabilities.

Theologies which enforce strict gender roles from an early age often claim that this is necessary to prevent the collapse of society. Claims may be made that the sexes are so ill-suited to each others' assigned tasks that disaster will occur if people are allowed to perform tasks outside of their assigned gender roles. Claims are also often made that this strict policing is ultimately "for your own good"—that people

---

13. Olson, K. R. (2017, September 1). When sex and gender collide. Scientific American. https://www.scientificamerican.com/article/when-sex-and-gender-collide/

who engage in cross-gender behavior end up unhappy or spiritually damaged as a result of coloring outside the lines.

Some Pagan theologies do have ideas about strict gender roles. Since "Pagan" is an umbrella term which covers hundreds of thousands of religious traditions which have existed throughout hundreds of thousands of years, some have become patriarchal, and a few have become matriarchal.

Modern Pagans however, most often believe that a cross-cultural study of Pagan gender roles proves that gender roles are overrated. Even among neighboring societies with violently enforced gender roles, for example, these enforced roles have often been so wildly different as to make it clear that neither was really based on an accurate understanding of male and female capacities.

The ancient Spartans and Athenians, for example, both violently enforced gender roles on a basis of biological sex. But Spartans believed that women should be physically strong and fit, and should be in charge of running businesses, managing property and wealth, and generally performing all the activities necessary to run society so that their men could focus their entire beings on becoming elite warriors.[14]

Athenians, by contrast, treated women almost exclusively as household servants and caregivers, believing that women were generally incapable of athletic or intellectual feats and that it was immodest for

---

14. Mark, J. J. (2023, July 29). Spartan women. World History Encyclopedia. https://www.worldhistory.org/article/123/spartan-women/

a woman to so much as leave her home unaccompanied by a male relative.[15]

Imagine the Athenians' horror and fascination when the Spartans occasionally sent female athletes to compete in regional athletic championships.

Meanwhile, on the other side of the Mediterranean, ancient Carthagians engaged in behavior which either Greek society would have found to be in grievous conflict with their own gender roles. Their society does not seem to have collapsed because their people were engaging in "cross-gender" behavior either; in fact, they gave the ancient Greeks and Romans such a run for their money that the Romans eventually imported a foreign goddess and her transfeminine priesthood specifically because she promised to turn the tide of their war against Carthage if they honored her and her clergy.[16]

Because the sweep of history seems to suggest that there are no truly infallible gender roles, modern Pagan communities tend to reject any enforcement of gender roles at all. In a theology which teaches that all people are divinely created and/or manifestations of the Divine unfolding itself into the physical world, the philosophy in many modern Pagan circles has become that the best way to optimize the realization of Divine will is to optimize the freedom of individuals to pursue their own, internally sensed Divine calling.

---

15. Gomme, A. W. (1925). The Position of Women in Athens in the Fifth and Fourth Centuries. Classical Philology, 20(1), 1–25. http://www.jstor.org/stable/262574

16. (1994). "The Roman and the foreign: the cult of the "great mother" in imperial Rome". In Thomas, Nicholas; Humphrey, Caroline (eds.). Shamanism, history, and the state. Ann Arbor: . pp. 164–190. . .

Without the preoccupation with maximizing childbirth and conditioning men to kill (see Chapter 7), societies both ancient and modern have appeared to take the approach that no two individuals are created alike, and that forbidding someone from pursuing their own perceived divine calling may be dangerous to society. Whereas some patriarchal societies fear God punishing them if they tolerate behavior which violates their laws about sexual and gendered activity, many Pagan societies which place the locus of divine revelation within the individual, have been known to fear divine punishment if they prevented individuals from fulfilling their own unique divine callings.

The hesitancy of young Pagans today to make universal statements about gender roles, and the enthusiasm of older Pagans for venerating the traditionally feminine gender roles that were demonized in their youth, has led to a number of intergenerational conflicts within modern Pagan communities. In some circles this conflict has become bitter, with older Pagans accusing younger Pagans of misogynistically rejecting feminine things and younger Pagans accusing older Pagans of trying to force them into accepting traditional gender roles.

It is my hope that we can move beyond these conflicts, and it is my belief that in order to do so we must understand each other's trauma.

It is difficult for young Pagans who never lived through a time when the demonization of women by men was a legal and religious norm to understand the fear of trans women and of younger Pagans "rejecting femininity" that is expressed by some older Pagans. It seems equally difficult for women who found healing in the veneration of the traditionally feminine to understand the fears of young Pagans who are deeply uncomfortable with having their spiritual identities equated with their reproductive organs or who feel that the image of a birth giving, caregiving Goddess as the supreme deity is just a repackaging of patriarchal gender norms.

On the other side of this debate is the world being cultivated by many young Pagans now. A world in which no gender expression is condemned or mandated, and assumptions about a person's spiritual nature are not made based on their anatomy.

The view of young Pagans is not that gender is unimportant; to the contrary, gender is considered a *very* important component of how someone experiences life and understands the world. For this very reason, younger Pagans generally refuse to make assumptions about a person's gender based on their reproductive anatomy, or about what sorts of activities a person should engage in based on their gender. If gender changes our embodied experience of the world, after all, having a diversity of gendered perspectives participating in every type of labor can only enrich our communities' knowledge and capabilities.

If we accept the idea that gender is much more than just biological reproductive potential, we must accept that it is intended for much more as well. If it changes our embodied experiences of life, our emotions, and the way we think about the world, we must accept that having a diversity of genders in a diversity of roles in our society is likely to yield a society whose knowledge is more complete, and whose abilities are more robust and adaptable to change and challenge.

Indeed, a growing body of scientific research suggests that diversity is an inherent strength in almost all aspects of biological life and behavior.[17] The idea that homogeneity—the pursuit of a single "ideal" model of gender, or a single "right" way of doing things—optimizes societal performance appears to be patently false.

---

17. Berg, N., Watanabe, Y. Conservation of behavioral diversity: on nudging, paternalism-induced monoculture, and the social value of heterogeneous beliefs and behavior. Mind Soc 19, 103–120 (2020). https://doi.org/10.1007/s11299-020-00228-2

So let us all consider adopting the view that divine callings come from *inside* the human soul, not from a written holy book. This view naturally leads to respect for individual gender identity and gender expression, which in turn leads to a world of marvelous diversity.

Chapter Seven

How Do Destructive Theological Ideas Arise?

Throughout this book, we have discussed theological ideas which have been used by our ancestors to ensure their survival, and which would allow us to solve many of our humanitarian and ecological crises. We have also discussed how these ideas have been systematically purged from Western culture, and to a large extent also from the imperial cultures of other regions of the world.

The remarkable thing is that many of these beneficial ideas have been independently purged many times over the course of the last few thousand years. In many cases, the societies that have actively eliminated reverence for nature and for all genders from their theologies and replaced them with theologies that treat living beings as tools with no meaningful legal or divine rights have had no common holy book or theology to guide them.

Why does this keep happening?

The answer is simple: greed.

In this chapter, I want to very briefly explore how these theological ideas which appear to have been espoused to some degree by our most ancient ancestors have repeatedly become demonized. Although our end goal is to explore the root causes of systemic violence against both our fellow humans and our fellow species, we will begin with a discussion of the rights of different genders, because the questions of respecting the rights and freedoms of human beings and respecting the lives of other species are deeply intertwined.

The Rise of Enforced Gender Roles

The archaeological record provides us with a wealth of information with which to study the evolution of gender roles over time, especially now that archaeology has advanced to the point that it is possible to make precise statements about an individual's gender and activities based on their remains. One of the most surprising things for many archaeologists over the last couple of decades has been the extent to which 20th century archaeology turned out to vastly overestimate the universality of gender roles in history.

In 19th and 20th century archaeology, it was so widely assumed that people of certain genders would be buried with certain kinds of grave goods that grave goods were actually used as determinants of the deceased's gender. Bodies buried with weapons were simply assumed to be men without any study of the skeletons themselves. In the same way, bodies buried with tools for making textiles were simply assumed to be women.

This turns out to have been wildly incorrect. With advances in understanding the role of hormones on skeletal development, as well as biochemical analysis of bones, modern archaeologists have been able to determine the biological sex of skeletons independent of their grave goods. And it turns out that the use of grave goods to determine the gender of ancient corpses was wrong between 30% and 50% of the time.

We now know that about a third of prehistoric warriors and large game hunters had ovaries.[1] [2] We have also identified at least one skeleton who was buried in the fashion typically used by their culture for women but who was biologically male.[3] [4]

The jury is out on how many of these graves represent looser ideas about gender roles by past societies and how many represent trans

---

1. Mayor, A. (2016). The Amazons: Lives and Legends of Warrior Women Across the Ancient World. Princeton University Pres.

2. Magazine, S. (2023, June 30). Early women were hunters, not just gatherers, study suggests. Smithsonian.com. https://www.smithsonianmag.com/smart-news/early-women-were-hunters-not-just-gatherers-study-suggests-180982459/#:~:text=But%20recent%20studies%20have%20increasingly,discovered%20buried%20alongside%20hunting%20weapons.

3. Gast, P. (2011, April 11). Scientists speak out to discredit "gay caveman" media reports. CNN. http://www.cnn.com/2011/WORLD/europe/04/10/czech.republic.unusual.burial/index.html

4. *Please don't let the title of the above article fool you - the "discrediting" was scientists discrediting the discovery of a "gay cave man" as many media outlets reported, when the skeleton was actually a Neolithic trans gender person.

gender individuals, since in most cases we don't have written records of their lives, much less their gender pronouns. But it seems likely that both factors were at play to some degree, since at least one burial of a person with testes was conducted using methods explicitly reserved for women, while some graves of warriors with uteruses are accompanied by inscriptions that do seem to suggest that they were socially considered women.

So how did several cultures move independently from an ancient past in which gender roles were broad and varied and trans gender identities were accepted as a reality, to a recent past in which trans gendered behavior was frequently punished and individuals were expected to shape every decision and behavior in their lives around adherence to strict gender roles?

One clue from the archaeological record is that gender roles seem to have become reliably more restrictive as time passed. Hunter-gatherer societies generally show the highest degrees of equality among all people. As humans organize themselves into large social units and develop an interest in conquering their neighbors for land and slave labor, inequality including class and gender inequality seem to appear and grow steadily more extreme. [5]

One argument that has been used to support patriarchal gender roles as natural or inevitable has been the great similarity of these gender roles among modern and imperial cultures. Yet we see from the archaeological record that these gender roles appear to be enforced almost exclusively in militaristic societies which highly prioritize conquest.

---

5. Flannery, K. V., & Marcus, J. (2014). The creation of inequality: How our prehistoric ancestors set the stage for monarchy, slavery, and Empire. Harvard University Press.

WORLD SOUL

While the details of these divisions of labor have varied widely across history, as we saw in the previous chapter, they all seem to follow two similar goals:

> 1. The optimization of people with uteruses as producers of soldiers and material support for armies.
>
> 2. The optimization of people with testes as fighting and killing machines.

Across imperial cultures, people with uteruses are often forced into the roles of conceiving and raising as many children as possible, while dedicating the rest of their existences to various activities that support armies full of warriors who don't have uteruses. This support can be as household servants in ancient Athens, as financiers in ancient Sparta, or as factory workers in America around World War II.

The logic of this arrangement for a society that prioritizes conquest is obvious. Only people with uteruses can make more soldiers, so if you want to grow your army and replace your dead soldiers as fast as possible, it makes sense to force them to do that as much as possible. And since people with testes *can't* have babies, it makes sense to force them to mold themselves into optimal killing machines.

In pursuit of conquest, then, people cease to be respected as individuals who experience inner divine callings, and are instead objectified as cogs in a war machine. The job of people with uteruses is to make as many babies as possible, and anyone who thinks differently is being misled by demonic forces. The job of people with testes is to impregnate women, then go out and fight and kill to expand their empire.

Anybody who argues with or resists this assumption is a danger to society; surely, if either sex wavers from their single-minded focus on their assigned tasks, the empire will collapse into anarchy.

Except, of course, we know from the study of history that none of that is true. The only human activity that departing from these gender roles seems to interfere with is the waging of constant war, since societies that fail to maintain male supremacy and toxic masculinity as enforced cultural standards do seem to begin to question whether they want to dedicate their lives to conquering other human beings and teaching their children to do the same.

I suppose that the cessation of endless war could be considered a "collapse of civilization" by the profiteers whose fortunes depend on warfare. These profiteers often often use their fortunes to run propaganda machines and support religious organizations that seem friendly to their cause in order to secure popular support to continue extracting wealth from the destruction of their fellow living beings.

This symbiotic ecosystem has become cartoonishly obvious in my own society in recent years; America's last Secretary of Education, who fought against efforts to make quality education more affordable and argued in favor of shunting students into conservative religious schools, was the sister of the founder of military contractor Blackwater Security[6] and the wife of the founder of a profit cult which preaches that profit is a sign of proper religious faith and generates billions

---

6. Mazzetti, M., & Goldman, A.. Erik Prince, Blackwater founder and Betsy Devos' brother, recruits ex-spies to infiltrate liberal groups - including campaigns and Unions. Chicago Tribune. https://www.chicagotribune.com/nation-world/ct-nw-nyt-erik-prince-spies-liberal-groups-20200307-6xcvuopzzzaahbwtdruzi3ytnm-story.html

of dollars by preying on people's insecurities about their ability to perform traditional gender roles.[7] [8]

The same presidential administration featured a Secretary of State who was also the CEO of an oil company which stood to profit both from Middle Eastern wars and from climate change denial,[9] and a Secretary of Energy who was the same Texas governor who oversaw the censoring of environmental science reports we discussed in Chapter 4.[10]

Perhaps it is no wonder that this administration subsequently attempted to remove all references to climate change and LGBTQ people from government websites, sent a gag order forbidding scientists from discussing environmental science findings with the public without government approval, and informed the CDC that grant propos-

---

7. Peterson-Withorn, C. (2019, August 1). Inside Betsy Devos' billions: Just How Rich is the Education secretary? Forbes. https://www.forbes.com/sites/chasewithorn/2019/07/24/inside-betsy-devos-billions-just-how-rich-is-the-education-secretary/?sh=71519d433b0e

8. This is my story. Amway is a religious cult. Reddit: The Front Page of the Internet.. https://www.reddit.com/r/antiMLM/comments/basst3/this_is_my_story_amway_is_a_religious_cult_im/

9. Shear, M. D.. (2016, December 13). Rex Tillerson, Exxon C.E.O., chosen as secretary of State. The New York Times. https://www.nytimes.com/2016/12/12/us/politics/rex-tillerson-secretary-of-state-trump.html

10. Murphy, T. (2016, December 13). Rick Perry's war on science. Mother Jones. https://www.motherjones.com/environment/2016/12/rick-perry-energy-secretary-climate-censorship/

als to research issues affecting women's reproductive autonomy and trans gender identities would not be funded.[11][12]

The patterns of profit-driven exploitation in human behavior are very clear.

Although I have used it throughout this book, I want to clarify the definition of "patriarchy" here. People often hear opposition to patriarchy as a matter of opposition of women to the rule of men, but as we have seen so far, this system is not that simple. It is a system which attempts to force both men and women into strict and oppressive gender roles, with men being given the illusion of power because they are allowed to use violence. The violence that is done to men's spirits under patriarchy is often denied on the basis that the behaviors and emotions that are forbidden to them are feminine and therefore bad, weak, and they are better off without them.

Under patriarchy, men and women alike are subject to having their every thought and feeling molded, policed, approved, or condemned by a structure of almost exclusively male leaders. In many global societies we see this both in politics and in religion, where patriarchy not only requires obedient subservience of women and children, but also forces men to destroy any "undesirable" thoughts or feelings within

---

11. Plait, P. (2017, January 25). Trump orders Gov't agencies to shut down social media, EPA to take down Climate Change Pages. Slate Magazine. https://slate.com/technology/2017/01/trump-issues-gag-orders-on-science-agencies.html

12. Sun, L. H., & Eilperin, J. (2023, April 9). CDC gets list of forbidden words: Fetus, transgender, diversity. The Washington Post.
https://www.washingtonpost.com/national/health-science/cdc-gets-list-of-forbidden-words-fetus-transgender-diversity/2017/12/15/f503837a-e1cf-11e7-89e8-edec16379010_story.html

themselves, often leaving them in states of emotional distress that can translate into violence toward women and children.[13]

This is what modern feminists mean when they say that patriarchy harms everyone, men and women alike. Patriarchy does not only refer to the control of men over women; it also refers to the painful control of men which is exerted by other men as part of a bid to maintain and preserve the power of the ruling class in a patriarchal society.

"Patriarchy" refers to the shaming of emotions in men, the shaming and silencing of male victims of violence and sexual harassment, and the pressure men face to become machines dedicated to the waging of war or the creation of profit at the expense of their spiritual wholeness and mental and physical well-being.

All of this is what feminists are referring to when they say they wish to "smash the patriarchy." Indeed, recent waves of feminism have featured a heavy emphasis on creating emotional and material support for male victims of violence and sexual harassment, and on embracing the "tender masculinity" which allows men to express their feelings of affection, sensuality, sadness, and other emotions which have often been rejected by patriarchal power structures who would prefer men to serve as engines of war or profit. Preliminary evidence seems to suggest that this is working: suicide rates among men have been found to drop by up to 50% in societies with high rates of feminism.[14]

---

13. How patriarchy and toxic masculinity hurt men. Therapist.com. (2023, July 11). https://therapist.com/society-and-culture/how-patriarchy-toxic-masculinity-hurt-men/

14. Evans, J. (n.d.). How does feminism benefit men?. The Courier Online. https://www.thecourieronline.co.uk/how-does-feminism-benefit-men/

The objections from critics that this constitutes a "feminization" or "emasculation" of men stem from the patriarchal idea that these aspects of the self should not exist in men, and that men are somehow becoming "less manly" if they are allowed to become spiritually whole. The same logic that spiritual wholeness is contrary to traditional gender roles is at play when women are accused of "rejecting femininity" when they embrace their anger and their abilities of economic productivity and self defense.

A major part of healing the wounds of patriarchy and allowing men, women, and children to heal and live as whole individuals instead of tools of war and profit is the placement of women and other genders in positions of power.

Because *no* women benefit from patriarchy, while a small percentage of men do, placing women in positions of power creates a high likelihood that these female religious and political leaders will oppose patriarchal oppression of both sexes. For this reason, electing female and transgendered political and religious leaders is a good investment in lessening the damage to the human soul and to the living world which occur as a result of patriarchal expectations.

Over time, imperial cultures tend to slot females away from financially productive support duties because it turns out that it's difficult to keep people in positions of subservience if they are able to pay their own way in the world. The stereotype that women are not suited to work outside the home or handle money arises, and it is challenged only in times of necessity brought on by war when there simply aren't enough men available to handle the economically productive labor.

For us, this trend arguably culminated in the late 19th or early 20th century, when many societies around the world considered practically all involvement by women in the public sphere to be immodest and inappropriate, and rejected the existence of any genders other than cis male and cis female as legitimate. This progression of oppression then began to rapidly decline in some societies in the early to mid-20th century as women began to organize en masse to demand equality.

What developments in human history have closely followed the same timeline as that of gender oppression? War, environmental destruction, and wealth hoarding. It is easy to argue from the historical record that all of these evils are driven by the same underlying motivation: greed.

Let's take a look at precisely how the glorification of wealth hoarding led to the demonization of most living beings on this planet, under the argument that respecting their rights would be a moral evil.

The Rise of Greed

In addition to gender equality, another major difference between hunter-gatherer societies we have been able to study and the later imperial societies, is their view of wealth and resources. Hunter-gatherer societies we have been able to study today tend to hold sharing to be the most basic social expectation, and have socially engineered punishments for those who hoard wealth or become egotistical about their contributions to the material prosperity of their tribe.[15]

Interactions are on record of several modern hunter-gatherer tribes with European explorers in which the Europeans expressed puzzlement at the fact that the tribes did not heap praise and adulation upon those who provided big game kills or other material boons. When asked, the hunter-gatherers expressed equal puzzlement that

---

15. Peterson, N. (1993). Demand Sharing: Reciprocity and the Pressure for Generosity among Foragers. American Anthropologist, 95(4), 860–874. http://www.jstor.org/stable/683021

the European societies did not have social customs in place to keep the egos of individuals in check and prevent those with great physical strength from oppressing others.[16]

This may go some way toward explaining why many indigenous tribes also reported puzzlement with the seemingly endless hunger of European explorers for material wealth, and why many Christian missionaries reported amazement to find that indigenous societies were better at caring for children, disabled, and elderly people through resource sharing than the Christian societies back home were.[17]

In the archaeological record, we see that at some point in the development of certain societies, wealth hoarding stopped being punished and began to be allowed or even praised. This did not immediately lead to the destruction of gender equality or respect for other species as living beings, but in most cases within a few millennia of beginning to glorify the accumulation of wealth these shifts had occurred.

Typically this shift was then followed within another few millennia by empire collapse due to a combination of ecosystem and food system collapse and strikes or violent revolts by workers and soldiers who no longer found that their societies rewarded them adequately for their work because the ruling class was taking all the rewards for themselves.

Does this cycle sound familiar to anybody?

I think you have the basic shape of the process by which patriarchy arises in theology, and why these theological changes tend to cause

---

16. Cogito. (2019, October 26). Who are the san bushmen? | the World's oldest people. YouTube. https://www.youtube.com/watch?v=1oQ5Jd7p2aY

17. Flannery, K. V., & Marcus, J. (2014). The creation of inequality: How our prehistoric ancestors set the stage for monarchy, slavery, and Empire. Harvard University Press.

humanitarian disasters. It may also be obvious to you by now why the glorification of greed and the objectification of humans as war machines would go hand-in-hand with the objectification of our fellow species as "natural resources" and ultimately their unsustainable exploitation.

But let's take just a moment to examine that progression together in detail.

The Demonization of Animism

It is important to note here that, as far as I'm aware, few world religious systems have punished animistic beliefs and practices. Christianity and Islam are, as far as I'm aware, the only religious systems which have condemned indigenous animistic practices as idolatry and devil-worship.

Certain atheist philosophies join the list when they teach that "excessive" regard for living beings and ecosystems is an impediment to progress, where "progress" is often defined as the conversion of natural resources into material wealth. As we mentioned in Chapter 4, both communist and capitalist societies have been known to censor science and literature which were deemed to turn public opinion against this conversion of living beings into economic power.

I note this because, unlike the enforced traditional gender roles of patriarchy, the full-on demonization of animism does not appear to be universal. Patriarchal religions exist which still formally permit animistic beliefs and practices, though these beliefs and practices are often disregarded when they stand in the way of profit motive, and an unfortunate side effect of secularization can be the painting of animistic beliefs and practices as ignorant superstition. This is of course very convenient for industrialists who wish to cut down forests.

It is easy to see why a ruling class might wish to do away with the concept of divinity in nature when wealth can only be extracted from natural resources through their destruction. It's instructive to study the history of gender relations, and human-animal relations in the Christian Bible and the history of Christian Europe in order to trace this development.

The first place within Christian texts where animals and plants are characterized as objects made explicitly for the use and pleasure of humanity is the Book of Genesis. While the Christian Old Testament is based on Jewish scriptures, it contains some very important omissions.

English translations of the Christian Bible omit six of the genders recognized by Judaism for purposes of religious law, and drastically strengthen both these dictated gender roles and this species supremacy. Christian translators specifically changed the original Hebrew language of Genesis to make Eve appear vastly more inferior to Adam, describing her as a "helpmeet made from Adam's rib," when the Hebrew word for "rib" appears nowhere in the original text and instead both Hebrew depictions show humanity being created as a nonbinary being which is then split into equal male and female halves by God.[18] The Jewish understanding that humans are given dominion over other species *only* so long as they earn the right by behaving righteous stewards[19] is also drastically changed.

---

18. Scheinerman, R. (2022, May 3). The eight genders in the Talmud. My Jewish Learning. https://www.myjewishlearning.com/article/the-eight-genders-in-the-talmud/

19. Neril, R. Y. (2017, February 25). Genesis and human stewardship of the Earth. My Jewish Learning. https://www.myjewishlearning.com/article/genesis-and-human-stewardship-of-the-earth/

One can speculate that these changes might have been related to the fact that these translations were standardized after Christianity's adoption as the official religion of a military empire. Indeed, some have speculated that the teachings Christianity inherited from Judaism, which were already more heteronormative and less animistic than those of the Roman Pagans, may have made Christianity an appealing religion for a martial Emperor to convert his empire to.

The new Christian religion had the support of the masses of people due to the more egalitarian teachings of the New Testament, which explicitly stated that people of all genders and social classes were equal children of God. But these teachings were almost immediately de-emphasized by the Christian leaders, who gained the blessing of the Roman Empire, with explicitly sexist translations of the Old Testament and new Christian theories about the Divine Right of the ruling class prevailing in organized religious education instead.

Teachings were quickly established that the salvation of one's soul depended entirely on following the rules of the imperial church, as individuals were deemed unable to perform soul-saving spiritual operations or learn soul-saving theology on their own. Christianity rapidly transformed from a religion of personal relationship with a loving God into a religion in which one's spiritual development had to be carefully controlled and directed by state-approved clergy or all hope of avoiding eternal torture in Hell was lost.

The new imperial translations of the Christian texts also provided unlimited license for the oppression of people with uteruses into childbearing support roles and the destructive exploitation of plants and animals, which would have been more difficult to justify under Roman Paganism where land spirits were recognized as beings powerful enough to require placating and many explicit models of female divine power and holy people of other genders were ingrained too deeply to be effectively removed.

In Christian Europe over the course of the next two thousand years, prioritization of conquest and the accumulation of wealth continued to advance. Wars were fought between different Christian sects over land and wealth, with rulers giving theological explanations about how their rivals were destroying the souls of their own people by teaching heretical and therefore damnable ideas.

Doctrines were written authorizing European explorers on other continents to claim the lands by any means necessary for their Christian rulers, on the grounds that the people populating these lands were Hellbound unless they converted to Christianity, so the colonizers were doing them a favor.[20] All animistic practices dedicated to maintaining the right relationship with the land and its non-human inhabitants were banned as "devil worship," which would result in condemnation to Hell and the disintegration of society if allowed to continue.[21]

Capitalists of recent centuries were happy to support the demonization of existing animistic practices because this condemnation opened more lands up for destruction. Numerous valiant attempts by American Indians to defend lands and ecosystems from destruction by profit-extracting enterprises were brought to bloody ends by settlers espousing Christianity and atheistic philosophies who claimed that

---

20. Doctrine of Discovery. The Gilder Lehrman Institute of American History. (n.d.). https://www.gilderlehrman.org/history-re sources/spotlight-primary-source/doctrine-discovery-1493

21. GotQuestions.org. (2007, August 14). Animism. GotQuestio ns.org. https://www.gotquestions.org/Animism.html

concern for the spirits of the land was superstitious ignorance at best and dangerous devil-worship at worst.

Even when modern scientists began to raise the alarm that ecosystem destruction and human-caused extinctions were reaching levels dangerous enough to threaten the future of our food web and our economy, these scientists were dismissed with charges that they were anti-Christian. Tenuous arguments were made, and believed by tens of millions, that it was "blasphemous" to suggest that humans were powerful enough to harm God's creation, or that it was "idolatrous" to support "nature worshippers" who "heretically" attributed real moral value to the lives of non-human beings. To this day, preachers exist who can be heard teaching that it is folly to try to preserve this flawed, temporary physical world forever or that "excessive" love for one's fellow living beings constitutes idolatry.

Now we stand at a crossroads. We know we are repeating the history of every empire before us, all of which have fallen due to a combination of unsustainable exploitation of nature and unsustainable exploitation of their own people. We have all the knowledge necessary to not only prevent a collapse, but create a better world for our children than humanity has ever known.

But will we do it? That's up to us.

Two Ways Forward

In many cases archaeologists are now beginning to conclude that, instead of vanishing from the face of the Earth, the peoples of these empires abandoned their cities en masse and began living off the land in surrounding areas. Many modern Pagans are now making serious efforts to do the same thing, finding that urban life is often economically unsustainable for the working class and that the risks posed by the widespread use of dangerous and unsustainable practices in mainstream food production are too great to bear. Unfortunately, we know that in most historic cases such shifts were not undertaken en masse until they were forced by famines and wars.

We have so far been gambling that our technology and enlightened values would save us from similar fates and allow our civilization to progress and develop indefinitely. While I agree that this would be a good outcome if our civilization continues the trend of the last century of eradicating disease and decreasing the numbers of those dying from war and hunger, at the time of this writing there are many signs that the American empire is following the trends seen in cases of previous catastrophic empire collapse.

Economic indicators such as wealth inequality are now at levels in the United States which are typically seen shortly preceding violent revolutions. Life expectancy and rates of higher education are on the decline due to refusal to invest in healthcare systems and scholarship on the part of the ruling class. Both left- and right-wing agitators are actively advocating for the overthrow of the U.S. government, and both camps have significant numbers of followers whose hatred of each other and of the current ruling class has been demonstrably rising for over a decade.

Elsewhere in the global community, multiple major world powers are seriously threatening land wars for territory against neighboring countries. Levels of people facing hunger and forced migration due to climate crises and complications of unsustainable agricultural practices have been growing rapidly for the past 20 years, reversing the trend of declining world hunger seen in the last decades of the 20th century.

The technology to alleviate all of these losses is at hand, as is the knowledge of psychology, history, and economics necessary to heal and reverse these damages. But we don't seem to be using it.

Past imperial collapses were accompanied by tragic losses. Lifespans were shortened for generations by famine and war due to environmental depletion and loss of organized defensive forces. Major losses of medical, scientific, technical, and historical knowledge occurred as societies ceased to produce enough excess wealth to support a scholar class. In many cases people gained more independence and autonomy by being out from under the boots of the ruling class, but at the cost of losing the benefits of large-scale cooperation.

Again, does this sound familiar to anybody?

Hope is not lost. We can hope that we can actually put our knowledge into practice and change our ways before it is too late. We can hope that, like some recent empires which fell back within their own borders, we can manage to begin rewarding our workers for their roles in our society sufficiently to avoid civil war. We can hope that we can use our scientific knowledge to repair the damage we have done to the web of life upon whom we depend for our own continued survival before it is too late to avoid mass famine.

Indeed, we have a pretty good idea of *how* to avoid a collapse and create a future for our children that is better than any era the world has ever known. But do we have the will to defy the powerful who profit off of our destruction and actually *do it*?

How do we curb the greed which treats humans and other living beings as nothing more than objects to be used in the pursuit of profit?

In one way, this is simple: adopting a worldview which values life over profit and recognizes all living beings as necessary contributors to the web of life is not complicated, because this reality is self-evident.

In another way, it is complicated. When our livelihoods depend on systems of power which are driven by greed, when we are surrounded by cultural conditioning that is driven by greed, and when we are faced with propaganda at every turn telling us that molding ourselves into machines for war and profit is the morally right thing to do, creating a new system to replace this prevailing system must be a multi-step process.

In this final chapter, we will look at a vision of what a society that values life first and foremost may look like. It is my hope that this vision will inspire some practical steps that we can all take, in accordance with our personal divine callings, to create a better world for our children and grandchildren instead of a worse one.

If we can work together and support each other in making these changes to our lives, progress toward building a survivable economy and a spiritually whole existence can be made astonishingly quickly. If we can motivate these changes through awareness of the theological importance of respect for life and freedom, so much the more fulfilling.

I will frame these suggestions from a standpoint of the Pagan theological ideas I have suggested in this book so far. But they are compatible with the core of most theologies, and are by no means only appropriate for Pagans. These suggestions will benefit anyone who values the life God has created more than the almighty dollar.

Chapter Eight

Building a Better World on Pagan Theology

When was the last time you felt really good? For me, I feel my best when I wake up naturally in the morning after sleeping with the windows open. The physical sensation of well-being and wholeness I get upon waking up with air that has been in communion with the local plants and animals sweeping over my body is remarkable and incomparable. I noticed this consistent effect as a child and have tried to replicate it ever since.

Unfortunately, this is often not possible in my local area. I have asthma—possibly due to a lack of communion with my bacterial kin as an infant[1] —and my neighborhood often has high levels of industrial dust and fumes in the air. This is true of almost all the urban population centers where most of humanity now lives. After a few summers featuring terrifyingly dense smog descending, I've taken to keeping an app on my phone which reports air quality measurements from monitoring stations around my city and sleeping with the windows open only on nights when dangerous particle counts are reasonably low.

On days when the air quality is good, I may go for a walk in the local park system after waking. I moved to this neighborhood, which I will explore as a model for a better future, for a number of reasons. One major requirement was the robust, two-mile-long stretch of public park land running along a river within walking distance. Another was good walkability and access to public transit, enabling me to get my daily needs met without owning a car. Yet another was the local culture of mutual aid and neighborly assistance, which we will discuss later.

I was astonishingly lucky to find all three in a neighborhood which did not require me to have a six-figure income to live in, since parks and public transit are usually more robustly funded in the United States in wealthy neighborhoods.

The local park is a thing of beauty, and a sign of hope. Local residents can volunteer to help with the cleaning, planting, and weeding of the park's curated ecology on regular dates when park staff show up

---

1. The hidden reason children born by C-section are more likely to develop asthma. Rutgers University. (n.d.). https://www.rutgers.edu/news/hidden-reason-children-born-c-section-are-more-likely-develop-asthma#:~:text=The%20researchers%20found%20that%20delivery,composition%20of%20the%20gut%20microbiota.

to supervise. The park is also an outpost for local scientists who study the flora, fauna, and local environmental conditions. The scientists host summer camp programs for local students over the summer to learn about what they do.

The park's stewards have wisely seeded it with native plants and wildflowers, including those that work together to naturally replenish the soil with each growing season and many which have edible and medicinal uses in addition to being beautiful. I make notes sometimes of which might be used as food in a food emergency, though I'm afraid this might end badly; it's almost certain that the soil around this river, like most soil in urban areas and in many suburban areas, is so contaminated with neurotoxins as a result of decades of industrial activity that it would cause cancer clusters in adults and brain and endocrine system damage in children if we were to begin eating food grown in it regularly. This is why the nearby community garden grows food in soil which must be imported and kept in elevated planters above the ground.

Still, there are signs of hope everywhere. This park system is particularly known for playing host to rare birds, to the point that bird watchers come from hundreds of miles around to observe the dizzying variety of songbirds and water birds who live here full-time or make this place a stop on their migratory routes.

Last year, a snapping turtle estimated to weigh almost 100 pounds was spotted nearby. The sight was so unusual that "Chonkasaurus" quickly became an Internet sensation, and this was both uplifting and heartbreaking. Chonkasaurus's mere existence here was inspiring because a few decades ago it would have been impossible for Chonky, and many of today's other park residents, to live here due to the high levels of pollution from human activity. In most places around the world wildlife is disappearing at an alarming rate, but in the places that used to be the worst it's beginning to come back.

I know that we could decrease levels of pollution, including that of the air, by more robustly funding public transportation to reduce people's need to rely on individual car trips in their daily lives. My city's public transit is some of the best in the United States, but commuting more than a mile or two away via bus still takes an average of one to two hours out of a person's daily schedule, and there is only one of the more time-effective rail lines running through this relatively outlying area.

We could also reduce every kind of pollution, including both the toxic particles in the air and the neurotoxins in the water and soil, by more strictly regulating industrial activities. This would cause massive political outcry because it would cut into the profit margins of the corporations which account for most of my country's economic activity. The profiteers would say these regulations were "job killers," claiming they'd be left with no choice but to eliminate hundreds of thousands of workers to pay for the regulations. This, of course, would be mostly untrue; most estimates show these companies' profit margins as being wide enough that the hit could come out of the profits of wealthy shareholders, not the paychecks of workers. But the wealthy shareholders will make arguments that they can't fund *other* businesses without those profits, and so it will go.

It is likely true that economic profits and GDP would drop in a world like the one I envision. It is also likely true that humans would be safer, more secure, happier, and more spiritually whole in such a world. Decreased corporate employment may not be such a problem if medical care and education were not run as extortionary for-profit industries in my society, if the need for medical care were lower because the environment were healthier, if people had more time and space and clean soil to grow their own food and cook for themselves, if certain predatory practices used by landlords and investors to squeeze high profit margins out of residential living spaces were banned.

Reduced dependence on corporate employment to meet our basic survival needs would increase both our community's physical security and our social and spiritual well-being. If people could grow food in community gardens and keep domestic livestock, if they could care for family members and neighbors in need instead of having to pay someone to do it for fear of losing their own paychecks, if they didn't need to pay for car ownership or regular treatment of asthma attacks from air pollution, we would all be happier.

Bhutan is the only country I know of that has ever undertaken to prioritize Gross National Happiness over GDP. The move, which makes tremendous sense to me, has been widely mocked and criticized by titans of industry and even certain theologians who have dragged out the old familiar arguments that happiness in this life is neither a realistic nor admirable goal, and that theologies and spiritual practices which promote it are idolatrous and wicked. One wonders if they are worshiping the creator, or the dollars.

The community garden is on my walking path home. It's an inspiring space, colorfully decorated by local volunteers and largely funded by local customers who can pay a modest fee to grow their own crops in generous planting spaces. Many of the local residents obtain their seeds from local heirloom seed swaps or small businesses which specialize in native and heirloom species, drastically increasing the biodiversity and therefore the resistance to environmental threats of our local food web.

Growing native crops in a polycrop fashion is not only more disease- and climate-resistant than the industrial monocrop agriculture which produces most of the food that we eat; when done skilfully it also requires far less use of chemicals that are toxic to farmers and ecosystems, sustainably enriches the soil, and provides a far better nutritional profile than the standard modern monocrop agriculture diets or processed food.

Everyone knows that this system is superior in its outcomes for all the living beings involved with it, and many people know how to do it; but it is rarely done, because it is less profitable than monocrop farming using toxic chemicals. Those foods which are most profitable on the modern global market are those which have the highest caloric yields per acre and which can be produced with the smallest possible amount of human labor. This precludes polycrop systems, which require considerable human labor to give individualized attention to separate species growing in the same spaces.

Herbicides and pesticides are widely used in today's most profitable food systems to minimize the loss of saleable crops and the amount of human labor needed to maintain the fields, and even chemical fertilizers are used in excess in an attempt to maximize productivity. These fertilizers then often leak into local water systems where they feed toxic algal blooms that strangle other forms of aquatic life and occasionally poison water supplies to the point that they become unsafe to drink during bloom season.

While some credit is due to GMO crops and certain artificial chemicals for helping to alleviate world hunger, the use of these technologies for the primary goal of maximizing profit is a major cause of ecosystem destruction, farmer poisoning, and global public health crises stemming from nutritional insufficiencies and unhealthy ingredients in our food. Palm oil is the most profitable fat which can be used to make processed foods feel rich and creamy; it is also a leading cause of both rainforest destruction and death from coronary artery disease.

Our obsession with profit is fatal. Greater reverence for the ecosystems we coexist with, and for our own bodies, may prevent this if it rose to the level of informing our activism, our votes, and our public policy.

In addition to allowing residents to grow food and medicinal plants, the space is used to train new arrivals from other countries in agricultural skills they might use to make a living. My neighborhood is also a major entry point for new immigrants, refugees, and asylum seekers coming to my city. I am convinced that this is largely responsible for the culture of mutual aid here, which far exceeds that of any neighborhood I have ever lived in.

Not long ago I was walking to the pharmacy. An older woman was visibly struggling to walk in the same direction, apparently suffering from some sort of chronic pain. I offered to walk her to the pharmacy, and she accepted. Along the way, three different people of different ethnicities stopped to see if she was alright, if she needed more help. When we arrived at the pharmacy—a locally owned operation staffed mostly by immigrants and children of immigrants—offered to deliver her medication to her home at no extra charge in the future, and snuck a free bag of surgical masks to protect against COVID into her bag.

Along the way, we passed fliers for the local mutual aid group. This completely volunteer-run organization has consistently shocked me with its effectiveness in offering local people assistance with procuring vital supplies like groceries, baby supplies, and COVID home tests. A local grocery store maintains an open gift card account for the group which shoppers can donate to at will, and offers a substantial discount on purchases made using this account. Local businesses and community events often allow the group's members to advertise and collect for their diaper drives, which bring in a steady flow of baby supplies that are then delivered by volunteers to families in need. Local churches and mosques both assist in the group's operations, as do local LGBTQ+ support organizations, and occasionally even the local government when the group is seen to be effectively addressing an acute need of local residents.

All of this can be done because neighbors have both the desire and the time to help each other. None of the people who run the group or perform its labor are paid or regulated by corporate or state sponsors. Local religious organizations do not exclude people or refuse to cooperate with groups based on differing theologies, and even political differences are ignored when the task at hand is providing concrete assistance to neighbors who are in acute distress.

Now, let us imagine a perfect world. One we are able to design from the ground up. How can we use this model, which has already been created by people who value life over profit or theological correctness, be expanded?

Evidence for the benefits of local park systems and nature areas is abundant. In addition to providing havens for non-human beings to thrive and grow, these clean our air and water, protect us from famines resulting from ecological collapse, and can even be used as emergency sources of food and medicine if their water and soil can be kept sufficiently free of human-generated pollution. They reduce crime and improve mental, physical, and spiritual health through communion with our fellow beings.

The drawback, of course, is that parks are generally not profitable. Their residents cannot be captured or killed and sold to the highest bidder, they cannot be used to grow profitable crops, and they cannot be developed into real estate that can be rented out for shelter at a profit of millions of dollars per year. Parks are affordable to maintain, but expensive in the sense of missed opportunities for financial gain. For this reason cities often treat park space as an expense, because maintaining them requires resisting high dollar offers from corporate developers who wish to use the land for profit.

Still, if I were in charge, half of our urban land area would be dedicated to this purpose. It would be interesting to observe what would happen if we instituted policies requiring city blocks to be interspersed with nature reserves of equal area. Such an endeavor would likely be supported by societies which espouse theologies which value our fellow living beings and the human quality of life on this Earth as intensely as our ancestors did, as intensely as indigenous peoples still do.

Perhaps not all of this area need be left to unspoilt wilderness. Perhaps some percentage ought to be devoted to community gardens which can teach agricultural techniques, including the care of helpful animals and sustainable polycrop agriculture with genetically diverse native and heirloom plant species. Such gardens would drastically increase our society's food security in the event of disruptions to global supply chains or global food production, in addition to improving physical health through improved access to healthy crops and improving physical, mental, and spiritual health through communion with the Earth and Her inhabitants.

Both science and worship could be conducted in the parks and gardens. Ecologists, environmental scientists, and agricultural scientists could collect information about local ecosystems and test new agricultural techniques in every neighborhood. We could reasonably expect such robust data collection to rapidly increase our knowledge of our fellow species, with potentially drastic benefits to fields including medical science and food security. Local children could study with these scientists as part of school programs preparing them for future careers in these fields.

Any religion which venerates the natural world could easily find communion with it—or with God, Goddess, or whatever terminology you prefer—in these spaces. If self-reports from Pagan communities are anything to go by, we could expect the frequency of profound personal religious experiences to rise if worship services were regularly held outdoors amid robust natural ecosystems.

Spiritual communion with all living beings, or with all of God's creation, could become a lived daily reality and could shape drastically improved mental health outcomes and more compassionate and ethical behavior. Outdoor religious sanctuaries which honor our natural world could serve as powerful reminders to our people to never again abandon our fellow living beings and risk our grandchildren's lives in the process.

Such a society would likely still need stricter regulations on the release of toxins into the environment by economic activities. This might mean a somewhat decreased availability of manufactured material goods and foods grown on other continents. Prices of material goods and imported foods might rise; employment might drop. But how many of us would complain if we could grow much of our own food, had free access to nature areas within walking distance for relaxation and community gatherings, no longer needed personal ownership of cars in order to access food, nature, and employment, and decreased work hours meant we had more time to live and work for ourselves and our neighbors?

Other problems in the complex web of interdependence that is the modern economy would still need to be solved. But experts have proposals, backed by data and modern technological capabilities, for how to solve all of them.

The question, then, is one of priorities. Will we prioritize financial profits which are overwhelmingly claimed as personal wealth by the very rich, or life-sustaining communion with our fellow living beings? Will we prioritize the production of manufactured goods, or the production of foods and living conditions which give us physical and spiritual life? Will we prioritize having money, or having time to spend with our loved ones and our good Earth?

I know which I prefer.

We all have opportunities to make decisions about how we live, what we consume, how we vote, and how we show up when religious and political policy decisions are being made. We all have opportunities to cultivate our own spiritual relationships with the land we live on, and act in defense of it when ecological destruction threatens.

I realized that many of us do not have the time or money to spend very much of either on resisting the systems of oppression we live within. For many in Pagan communities, this has meant cultivating radical departures: I've had three different colleagues in religion move to rural areas where land is cheap and relatively unpolluted to start farms, in order to avoid the necessity of dedicating their lives to working for destructive corporations.

One major dilemma for modern Pagan leaders is this: do we drop out of a society that we know is destructive and begin to build our own communities in areas where land is still affordable and relatively nontoxic, or do we stay in urban centers where the majority of humans live and the majority of economic decisions are made?

I think the answer, ultimately, is "both." Rural Pagan communities provide havens for our fellow humans who cannot afford the costs of living in cities and who desire to dedicate their lives to cultivating harmonious relationships with our fellow beings. Urban Pagan communities provide havens for activists who may be able to influence the policies under which the majority of human living and economic activity are performed. Networking the two together holds the potential to provide the best of both worlds, linking the labor and economic autonomy available in rural communities with the needs and the opportunities to influence culture and policy which are available to urban Pagans.

A growing number of religious leaders would argue that such activism and communion with the Earth is becoming increasingly acceptable in other popular Western theologies.

I was pleasantly surprised, when writing this book, to discover that a huge percentage of American conservative Christians have stopped denying that climate change and environmental destruction are problems in recent years, and have turned their attention to Biblical teachings about good stewardship and the status of the Earth as ultimately belonging to God, not humanity. It seems that disagreement over whether environmentalism constitutes "Satanic idolatry" or fits the Biblical mandate to serve as good stewards of the land God gave us to tenant is now a major source of controversy within the same Christian denominations which just a few short years ago voted overwhelmingly to elect the most anti-environment politicians America had seen in a generation.

There is cause for hope. We can all do our part to grow that hope. But it is important that we do something.

We stand at a crossroads. Which path, and which theology, will we choose?

Customer reviews are important to the success of independent authors and small publishers. Books with more reviews are more likely to be stocked by bookstores, and more likely to be advertised to new readers by sales algorithms.

Please take a moment to review this book on the book review platform or book retailer site of your choice.

You can sign up to support Catherine Carr's work and receive perks at:

You can also sign up for Catherine's mailing list for free at:

Acknowledgements

All books are the work of many hands, and I am deeply indebted to those who helped bring me to the point where this book became possible.

Countless thanks to Twila York, Colleen McGee, and Damian Han for believing in me. Without your encouragement I may never have found my voice.

Thanks to Holli Emore, who welcomed me into Cherry Hill Seminary. Thanks to my seminary mentors, Heaven Walker and Dr. David Oringderff for encouraging me and offering their wise counsel. Ours are paths rarely taken, and you have been invaluable traveling companions on this journey.

Thanks to all of the helpers of the Village Dream Temple and Mystery School. Most especially to rain crowe, Luna Crow, and the Spell Weavers for creating a container for real magic. You were the first to show me that a better way of living truly is possible in this world despite the forces of greed.

Thanks to the Fire Fam for showing me that magic is real, and for getting me out to Portland. Thanks especially to Jess for her academic advice, to Solveig for doing the gods' work, to Reese for hosting us all, and to Winter for trying to teach me Sumerian.

Thanks to Kia LaFey of the Toronto Goddess Temple for being the first to validate my vision. Thanks to the Toronto Circle of Hope for showing me new ones, and the Wiccan Church of Canada for showing me a new vision of religious community. Thanks to Spirit who accompanied me to both—I miss you.

Many thanks are due to my editor, Izu Speilman, who has been both a source of relentless encouragement and a very knowledgeable source. Your knowledge of language and your valuable perspectives never cease to amaze me.

Last but never least, thanks to the Lady for calling me and to Loki for saving me. You give us our lives and this beautiful world.

About the Author

Catherine Carr earned her B.S. in Neuroscience from the University of Michigan in 2011 and worked in clinical research for five years before leaving the field to become a full-time writer. Her writings on religion and spirituality have appeared in *The Wild Hunt, The Crazy Wisdom Community Journal, Isis-Seshat, Bodhi! Bodhi! Bodhi!* and more.

She became a student of Cherry Hill Seminary and the Village Mystery Temple and Dream School in 2020. She now offers life coaching from a spiritually-oriented perspective, ritual facilitation, and quarterly classes for those seeking to deepen their spiritual community work and their personal practices.

Made in United States
North Haven, CT
16 October 2024